A Preference Hierarchy Model of Same-Turn Repair Operations in Talk-in-Interaction

Pragmatic Interfaces

Series Editors:

Enikő Németh T., University of Szeged

Dániel Z. Kádár, Dalian University of Foreign Studies, China and Hungarian Academy of Sciences

Károly Bibok, University of Szeged

In the last two decades it has become increasingly clear that language and language use cannot be studied separately and independently of each other. This new approach assumes an interaction between grammar (phonology, morphology, lexicon, syntax and semantics) and pragmatics. An analysis of the interfaces between each component of grammar and pragmatics (the 'interface view') can also be applied to hard-pragmatics and soft-pragmatics research. Hard-pragmatics studies the field of language use from philosophical, linguistic and logical points of view, while soft-pragmatics explores phenomena of language use from a social and socio-cultural perspective.

The definitions hard- and soft-pragmatics, adopted around the 1980s, have become somewhat dated since pragmatics has become a field of its own, and so these two trends have merged to some extent. Also, various pragmaticians made important attempts to blend these approaches. Nevertheless, a border between these areas continues to exist: hard-pragmaticians rarely venture into socio-pragmatic issues, and, vice versa, soft-pragmatic studies rarely make use of formal tools of hard-pragmatics.

Pragmatic Interfaces fills an important knowledge gap in the field of pragmatics as the first major publication project devoted to studying grammar–pragmatics interfaces and merging of soft-pragmatics with hard-pragmatics. Through this merging many pragmatic phenomena could be essentially revisited. Pragmatic Interfaces follows an interdisciplinary approach, allowing scholars from different areas of grammar and pragmatics to collaborate.

Published:

Data and Argumentation in Historical Pragmatics: Grammaticalization of a Catalan Motion Verb Construction
Katalin Nagy C.

Face and Face Practices in Chinese Talk-in-Interaction: A Study in Interactional Pragmatics
Wei-Lin Melody Chang

Implicit Subject and Direct Object Arguments in Hungarian Language Use: Grammar and Pragmatics Interacting
Enikő Németh T.

Impoliteness in Corpora: A Comparative Analysis of British English and Spoken Turkish
Hatice Celebi

Metapragmatics of Attentiveness: A Study in Interpersonal and Cross-cultural Pragmatics
Saeko Fukushima

Politeness Phenomena across Chinese Genres
Edited by Xinren Chen

A Preference Hierarchy Model of Same-Turn Repair Operations in Talk-in-Interaction

Zsuzsanna Németh

SHEFFIELD UK   BRISTOL CT

Published by Equinox Publishing Ltd

UK: Office 415, The Workstation, 15 Paternoster Row, Sheffield, South Yorkshire S1 2BX

USA: ISD, 70 Enterprise Drive, Bristol, CT 06010

www.equinoxpub.com

First published 2021

British Library Cataloguing-in-Publication Data

A catalogue record for this book is available from the British Library.

ISBN-13 978 1 78179 845 4 (hardback)
         978 1 78179 846 1 (ePDF)
         978 1 80050 040 2 (ePub)

Library of Congress Cataloging-in-Publication Data

Names: Németh, Zsuzsanna (Linguist), author.
Title: A preference hierarchy model of same-turn repair operations in
     talk-in-interaction / Zsuzsanna Németh.
Description: Sheffield, South Yorkshire ; Bristol, CT : Equinox Publishing Ltd, 2021. |
     Series: Pragmatic interfaces | Based on the author's dissertation (doctoral)—
     Szegedi Tudományegyetem (Hungary), 2016. | Includes bibliographical references and
     index. | Summary: "This book studies four self-initiated same-turn repair strategies in
     talk-in-interaction relative to each other, namely, recycling, replacement, insertion, and
     aborting"—Provided by publisher.
Identifiers: LCCN 2020052852 (print) | LCCN 2020052853 (ebook) | ISBN 9781781798454
     (hardback) | ISBN 9781781798461 (pdf) | ISBN 9781800500402 (epub)
Subjects: LCSH: Correction of speech errors. | Conversation analysis—Research—Methodology.
Classification: LCC P37.5.S67 N35 2021 (print) | LCC P37.5.S67 (ebook) | DDC 401/.9—dc23
LC record available at https://lccn.loc.gov/2020052852
LC ebook record available at https://lccn.loc.gov/2020052853

Typeset by JS Typesetting Ltd, Porthcawl, Mid Glamorgan

This book is dedicated to the memory of my grandmother,
Terézia Kollár

Contents

Figures

Tables

Acknowledgments

The beginnings of the research presented in this book date back to 2010, when I started to study the phenomenon of repair in conversation. I am indebted to Ágnes Lerch, whose conversation analysis seminar at the Department of General Linguistics, University of Szeged, Hungary, focused my attention on the possibilities of exploring naturally occurring talk with scientific methods. She was my first mentor, who suggested this topic to me for research and with whom I made the recordings of the SZTEPSZI corpus. I would like to thank the Institute of Psychology, University of Szeged, for making it possible to record nine conversations, and Mária Gósy for putting eight conversations from the BEA database at my disposal.

The main part of my research has been conducted under Enikő Németh T.'s supervision. Without her careful guidance and love over the past ten years not only would this book not have come into being, but I would not be who I am today.

I am also grateful to my other professors at the Doctoral School of Theoretical Linguistics, University of Szeged, especially to István Kenesei, Márta Maleczki, Lívia Ivaskó, and Krisztina Polgárdi.

After the doctoral school, for a year my research was supported by the TÁMOP-4.2.2/B-10/1-2010-0012 project. I conducted the main part of my research and wrote this book in the MTA-DE-SZTE Research Group for Theoretical Linguistics at the Universities of Debrecen and Szeged, where I have been working since 2013. I wish to thank András Kertész, the lead researcher of the group, for his encouragement and support, and for getting me involved in the metatheoretical study of linguistic theorising, which made me look at my object theoretical research with different eyes. Our discussions with my colleagues in the research group, Károly Bibok, Katalin Nagy C., Enikő Németh T., Csilla Rákosi, Marianna Varga, and Zoltán Vecsey, have not only formulated my ideas on linguistics, but also made our travels to Debrecen and several conferences throughout the world enjoyable and unforgettable.

At the Department of General Linguistics, University of Szeged, where I have been teaching since 2013, I can always rely on the help of my colleagues and friends Tibor Szécsényi, Katalin Nagy C., Anett Árvay, Eszter Bártházi, Boglárka Komlósi, Patrícia Balázs, and Marianna Varga, who have provided me with a loving, supporting, and inspiring atmosphere over the years.

My special thanks are due to Enikő Tóth and Tamás Péter Szabó for their insightful comments and constructive criticism on my doctoral dissertation *Four Repair Operations in Hungarian Conversations in the Light of Cross-linguistic Examinations*, which served as the basis for the present book.

I am grateful to the audiences at the conferences I have spoken at for their questions and comments, and the reviewers of my earlier papers on same-turn self-repair for their comments and suggestions, which helped me to develop my ideas in the various phases of my research.

I would like to thank Elsevier for their kind permission to reuse materials from the following paper (Copyright Elsevier):

Németh, Zsuzsanna (2012) Recycling and replacing repairs as self-initiated same-turn self-repair strategies in Hungarian. *Journal of Pragmatics* 44(14): 2022–2034.

I would also like to thank de Gruyter Mouton for their kind permission to reuse materials from the following paper (Copyright de Gruyter Mouton):

Németh, Zsuzsanna (2017) The interactional functions of four repair operations in Hungarian. In Stavros Assimakopoulos (ed.) *Pragmatics at its Interfaces – Mouton Series in Pragmatics 17.* 279–310. Berlin: Mouton de Gruyter.

I am grateful to the series editors Enikő Németh T., Károly Bibok, and Dániel Z. Kádár at Equinox. I also express my gratitude to Janet Joyce, Valerie Hall, and Steve Barganski for their assistance in the publishing process, and George Seel, Mónika Fischer, and Anna Fenyvesi for improving my English.

Finally, I cannot express in words how grateful I am to my family, my late grandmother Terézia Kollár, my father Ferenc Németh, my mother Ilona Fejős, and my brother Ferenc Németh for their constant love with which they supported me throughout my long years of education. One could not wish for a better father, mother, and brother.

Transcription conventions (Jefferson 2004)

.	Falling terminal contour
,	Continuing contour (incomplete)
?	Strongly rising terminal contour
-	Abrupt halt
[ ]	Overlapping speech
=	Latching (contiguous stretches of talk)
(0.7)	Pause measured in tenths of a second
(.)	Pause timed at less than 0.2 seconds
___	Stress on the word/syllable/sound
:	Lengthening of previous sound
CAPS	Increase in volume
° °	Decrease in volume
↑↓	Significant rise or fall in intonation
> <	Faster than surrounding talk
< >	Slower than surrounding talk
.hhh	Audible inhalation (the more *h*'s, the more aspiration; the dot may be raised as well; Sidnell 2010)
( )	Unintelligible speech
(( ))	Comments, e.g., quality of speech
¿	Rise stronger than a comma but weaker than a question mark (Sidnell 2010)

Abbreviations

1	first person
2	second person
3	third person
ABL	ablative
ACC	accusative
ADE	adessive
ADJDER	suffix deriving from an adjective
ALL	allative
CAU	causative
COM	comitative
COND	conditional
DAT	dative
DEL	delative
ELA	elative
GEN	genitive
ILL	illative
IMP	imperative
INE	inessive
INF	infinitive
INS	instrumental
PL	plural
POSS	possessive
PVB	preverb
SG	singular
SUB	sublative
SUP	superessive
TERM	terminative

CHAPTER 1

Introduction

1.1 The phenomenon of repair in conversation

In conversations, speakers may encounter problems which make them stop their talk-in-progress. The treatment of such problems which trigger speech disfluencies has been intensively studied in various linguistic disciplines. In the framework of conversation analysis, which studies human social interaction across sociology, linguistics, and communication (Stivers and Sidnell 2013: 1), the practices whereby a speaker interrupts the ongoing course of action in order to attend to possible trouble in speaking, hearing, or understanding the talk constitutes the domain of repair (Kitzinger 2013: 229) and is regarded as one of the fundamental structures of conversation (Sidnell and Stivers 2013: v). While conversation analysis examines repair from an interactional point of view, psycholinguistics regards repair as the correction of speech disfluencies (Gósy 2004: 15) and focuses on the cognitive aspects of the phenomenon.[1] The motivation of the research presented in this book is rooted in the interactional aspects of the repair mechanism: the question the present study seeks to answer is whether it is possible to examine the various self-repair operations that speakers execute in conversational interaction relative to each other. Therefore, I chose conversation analysis as the starting framework for my investigation.

Repair is composed of three parts in the conversation analytic framework: repair initiation, trouble-source, and repair outcome (Schegloff, Jefferson, and Sacks 1977; Schegloff 1997, 2000) (see Example (1)[2]).

(1) (SZTEPSZI2: 953)

```
01 Gábor:  de    hogy   egy   egy   poén        kedvéért     fölál-  ö
           but   that   a     a     joke        for.the.sake sacri-  uh
           'but for a joke do you sacri- uh
```

02	***kockára***	***teszed***	*egyébként*	*a:?*
	cube.SUB	put.2SG.DEF	by.the.way	the

risk, by the way, your (place at the university)?'

The cut-off in the word *fölál-*, which is obviously the first half of *föláldozod* 'you sacrifice', is a potential disjunction with the immediately preceding talk, therefore it is a repair initiation (Schegloff 2000: 207). The segment of talk to which the initiation of repair is addressed is the trouble-source or repairable[3] (Schegloff et al. 1977: 363). In Example (1) the segment that turns out to be problematic for the speaker is *fölál* 'sacri'. Gábor replaces it with *kockára teszed* 'risk', which will be the repair outcome. The repair outcome can be the solution or abandonment of the problem (Schegloff 2000: 207; cf. Schegloff et al. 1977: 364). Repair initiation and the repair outcome together are called the repair segment (Schegloff et al. 1977: 365). The term *repair* refers to the success of the repair procedure (Schegloff et al. 1977: 363).

While self-repair (self-initiated repair) is initiated by the speaker who produces the trouble-source (Kitzinger 2013: 230), other-repair (other-initiated repair) is initiated by someone other than the speaker of the repairable (Kitzinger 2013: 231). In Example (1), Gábor replaced the segment *fölál* 'sacri' with the word *kockára teszed* 'risk', therefore, he was the one producing the repairable and also the one who initiated the repair, which means that in Example (1) we have seen a self-repair. In contrast, let us consider Kitzinger's (2013: 232) example (Example (2)) where Angela initiates repair by using the format 'Pardon' in line 4. Here Angela indicates that the previous turn is not clear for her, consequently, the repair is initiated by someone other than the one who produces the trouble-source, which is an other-initiated repair.

(2) (Kitzinger 2013: 232)

1	Clt:	.hhhhh But it nourished him (.) in utero
2		well did it.
3		(.)
4	Ang:	**Pardon?**
5	Clt:	It nour- The placenta nourished him
6		.hhh in utero
7	Ang:	Yeah

Previous studies in the conversation analytic literature have paid a great deal of attention to self- and other-initiated repair.[4] Apart from English, repair has been studied across a range of other languages. Kitzinger (2013: 229) mentions Brazilian Portuguese (Guimaraes 2007), East Caribbean English Creoles (Sidnell 2008), Finnish (Laakso and Sorjonen 2010), French (Maheux-Pelletier and Golato

2008), German (Egbert 1996, 2004), Indonesian (Wouk 2005), Japanese (Fox et al. 1996; Hayashi 2003), Korean (Kim 1993, 2001), Mandarin (Wu 2006; Luke and Zhang 2010), Norwegian (Svennevig 2008), Russian (Bolden, Mandelbaum, and Wilkinson 2012), and Thai (Moerman 1977). While Fox and her seven colleagues (2009) have carried out a cross-linguistic study on self-repair in English, Bikol, Sochiapam Chinantec, Finnish, Indonesian, Japanese, and Mandarin (see Section 6.3), Fox, Maschler, and Uhmann (2010) have examined self-repair in English, Hebrew, and German. Self-repair is preferable to other-repair (Schegloff et al. 1977), and the most common type of repair is self-repair in the turn containing the repairable, i.e., same-turn self-repair (Kitzinger 2013: 232). The focus of this book is on this repair type.

Schegloff (2013) describes ten main same-turn repair operations that speakers carry through in order 'to deal with some putative trouble-source in an ongoing turn-at-talk in conversation or to alter it in some interactionally consequential way' (Schegloff 2013: 43). These repair operations are recycling, replacing, deleting, searching, parenthesising, sequence-jumping, reformatting, reordering, inserting, and aborting. Although the present book studies only four of these (replacing, recycling, inserting, and aborting), let us briefly consider all of them.

Replacing refers to the repair operation in which a speaker substitutes for a partially or wholly articulated element another, different element (Schegloff 2013: 43). In Example (3), Shelley replaces 'm-' with 'a lot of it'.

(3) (Schegloff 2013: 44)

Shl: that's why he can't go:, .hh an I said b- to be
   real <u>hon</u>est with you: <u>I</u> have to decide do I wanna
   spend this money becuz if <u>Mark </u>was goin .hh he was
   gonna pay fer- fer **m- a lot of it,** cause he won money
   playing footba:ll.

Inserting is an operation whereby the speaker interrupts the progressivity of the turn and, instead of articulating the next element due, s/he inserts one or more new elements into the turn-so-far (Schegloff 2013: 45) In Example (4), Stan lengthens 'f' then goes back and adds the adverb 'exactly' to modify the adjective 'funky'.

(4) (Schegloff 2013: 46)

Stan: And fer the <u>ha</u>:t, I'm lookin fer somethi:ng uh a
   little <u>diff</u>erent. Na- uh:f: not **f:: exactly f**unky but
   not (.) a r-regular type'a .hhh >well yihknow I I<
   <u>h</u>ave that other hat I wear. yihknow?
Joy: Yeah,

The speaker may abandon what s/he has said altogether and start the same action in a different form. This is the repair operation of *aborting* (Schegloff 2013: 52). Example (5) contains two aborting operations.

(5) (Schegloff 2013: 53)

She: Who ws the girl that was outside (his door¿)
        (0.8)
Mrk: Debbie.
        (0.8)
She: Who's Debbie.
Mrk: (Katz.)
        (0.7)
Mrk: **She's jus' that girl thet: uh:, (0.2)**
        ˙hh I <u>met</u> her through uh:m::, (1.0)
        I <u>met</u> 'er in <u>We</u>stwood.

When Sherrie cannot identify who Debbie is, Mark tries to refer to the woman in a different way ('She's jus' that girl thet:'). However, he interrupts the ongoing turn-constructional unit (TCU) and launches another attempt: he tries to describe how he met Debbie ('I met her through'). Then he interrupts this effort as well and refers to the place where he met Debbie ('I met 'er in <u>We</u>stwood').

The term *recycling* means that a co-interactant repeats a certain stretch of talk. Recycling has various uses, among which is its use as a repair operation when, for example, the speaker repeats some stretch of talk in order to say it in the clear in the case of overlapping talk (Schegloff 2013: 59). This happens in Example (6), where Kay repeats exactly that part of speech that overlapped with the other speaker's talk. The repair thus treats the potentially compromised hearing of 'I don think they grow a'.

(6) (Schegloff 2013: 59)

Rbn: Takes a   [bout a week to grow a culture,]
Kay: [**I don think they grow a**   ] **I don think they –grow a**
                   culture to do a biopsy.

When the speaker employs *deleting*, s/he deletes one or more elements which s/he has already articulated. In Example (7) Bee deletes 'als', that is the beginning of the word 'also', according to Schegloff (2013: 48).

(7) (Schegloff 2013: 48)

Bee: tuh go en try the:re. Because **I als- I tried** Barnes
        'n Nobles 'n, (0.6) they didn' have any'ing <u>they</u> don'
        have any art books she tol' me,

Ava: Mmm

The target of *searching* can be a name or a place, but it can also happen that the source of the problem is unclear, and the target is not 'precise' (Schegloff 2013: 50). In Example (8), the speaker searches for the name of a place, the Plaza Theatre.

(8) (Schegloff 2013: 49)

Joy: Why don'tchoo: go into Westwoo:d, (0.4) and go to
        <u>B</u>ullocks.
        (1.2)

Stn: Bullocks? ya mean that one **righ<u>t</u> u:m (1.1) tch! (.)
        right by thee: u:m (.) whazit the <u>P</u>laza? theatre::=**

Joy: =Uh huh,

Parenthesising is the interpolation of a clausal unit into the turn (Schegloff 2013: 51). In Example (9), Mike is telling a story and inserts some extra information about the character into the main line of the story.[5]

(9) (Schegloff 2013: 52)

Mik: [But in ne <u>mean</u>time it'd cost Keegan three spo:ts'nnuh
        <u>fea</u>ture.

Cur: Yeah¿

Mik: So, <u>b</u>oy when <u>Keeg</u>'n come in he- **yihknow how he's gotta
        temper anyway,** he js::: °wa:::::h sc [reamed iz damn
        e:ngine yihknow,   [

Cur: [Mm

Schegloff (2013: 64) distinguishes between first- and second-order repair operations. He regards replacing, inserting, deleting, searching, recycling, aborting, and parenthesising as first-order operations because they are deployed to do a basic, prima facie job on the turn-in-progress which each of them names. However, the names of second-order operations (sequence-jumping, reordering, and reformatting) refer to special jobs that first-order repair operations may be used to bring off. That is to say, we could understand second-order repair operations in the terminology of first-order operations, but in that case we would miss the real job the operation is used to accomplish. First-order operations in this sense can be the vehicles for second-order operations. When the speaker employs *sequence-jumping,* for example, s/he turns to something unrelated to the turn and sequence in progress (Schegloff 2013: 56). Therefore, it is similar to aborting. In Example (10), when Frieda notices a piece of woven material, she shifts from one sequence to another, which accomplishes a totally different action.

(10) (Schegloff 2013: 56)

Fre: You know what we're gonna- in fact I'm- she I
       haven't seen her since I spoke to you but I'm going to
       talk to=**what a you making?**
       (0.2)
Kat: It's a –bla:nket.
Fre: Did yu weave tha [t yourse:lf]
Kat: [I w o : :   ]ve this myself.=

Similarly, in Schegloff's next example, the replacing is a vehicle for a second-order operation, namely, a *reformatting.* Treating it as a replacing, however, would fail to grasp the perspectival change the repair is used to bring off. For instance, in Example (11), when Mom replaces 'I: would' with 'that would' she shifts the perspective from her personal feelings in connection with Virginia's offer to the offer itself.

(11) (Schegloff 2013: 63)

Mom: If I could see what you did with your money,
       (0.3)
Vir: You want me to write you a: a little list; every
          w[eek(?)
Mom: [I: would- (.) **that would** be great.

Reordering, which we could also analyse as a replacing repair, re-orders the elements of the TCU. In Example (12), when Bea realises that the elements in her TCU are out-of-order, she re-orders them and says 'js' never'.

(12) (Schegloff 2013: 65)

Bea: Ah hah end yih **never jus'** (.) eh yih **js' never** saw
       such devotion in your li:fe

Apart from Schegloff's (2013) study on these ten repair operations, there are also other works in the literature in the framework of conversation analysis focusing on same-turn repair operations in their own right. For example, while

Luke and Zhang (2010) and Wilkinson and Weatherall (2011) explore inserting in Mandarin Chinese, and in British, New Zealand, and U.S. English, respectively, Fox et al. (2009) and Fox et al. (2010) examine recycling and replacing in English, Bikol, Sochiapam Chinantec, Finnish, Indonesian, Japanese, and Mandarin, and English, Hebrew, and German, respectively. Németh (2012) focuses on recycling and replacing in Hungarian, and O'Neal (2015) on deletion and inserting in English as a lingua franca in Japan.

1.2 The aim and structure of the book

Although neither Fox et al. (2009) nor Fox et al. (2010) explore the frequency of recycling and replacing in their corpora, their collections of self-repair instances contain many more recycling than replacing repairs in all the examined languages in both studies (cf. Fox et al. 2009: 63; Fox et al. 2010: 2490). On the basis of this research, which involves a total of nine languages in their examinations, it can be suggested that recycling is a more frequent same-turn repair operation than replacing in all the languages examined. This prompts us to ask the following questions: Is there a cross-linguistic difference between the frequency of recycling and replacing? If so, how could we account for this? This latter question brings with it another, which is perhaps the most exciting: Is it possible to analyse and interpret same-turn repair operations relative to each other? The motivation and general aim of this book is to find an answer to this question.

Since it aims to explore recognisable social actions as they actually occur, that is, to empirically provide an account of what speakers accomplish in interaction (Schegloff 1996: 167), conversation analysis seems to be an ideal starting framework for my research. Conversation analysis grounds its empirical analyses in audio and video recordings of naturally occurring interactions collected in familiar, everyday settings as well as in institutional settings and regards these recordings as data (Mondada 2013). In order to answer my research questions, however, I need a wider spectrum of sources. Apart from semi-spontaneous speech recorded in a corpus consisting of casual face-to-face conversations in Hungarian, I build my argumentation on previous research, as well as on my intuition. The combination of these sources should be carried out in a careful way. Therefore, I also offer a metatheoretical reflection on my study using Kertész and Rákosi's (2012, 2014) *p-model of plausible argumentation*, which regards data as plausible statements originating from direct sources (e.g., corpus, linguistic intuition, and experiment) (Kertész and Rákosi 2012: 169) and makes the conscious integration of the data from these various data sources possible. In this book, following the terminology of the p-model, by the term *data* I mean plausible statements originating from direct sources, and not the recordings which conversation analysis researchers produce as data by collecting them for the purpose of studying them, and not the recordings which can be made by participants for their practical purposes and turned into data by researchers (Mondada 2013: 38). The p-model as a metatheoretical model of linguistic argumentation and data handling helps me to reflect consciously and metatheoretically on various subphases of my research, including the clarification of the most important concepts I work with during my study and the treatment of problems I encounter during my argumentation. Illuminating these metatheoretical issues during my object theoretical discussion, I aim to make my object theoretical results more reliable.

Since recycling and replacing have been investigated in respect of the same factors,[6] and in areally and typologically diverse languages in the studies mentioned above, and their use shows underlying universal tendencies (Fox et al. 2009: 80), exploring these two same-turn repair operations relative to each other seems to be an ideal first step for my investigation. First, in order to extend the cross-linguistic investigation of Fox et al. (2009) and Fox et al. (2010) to another language, I will examine Hungarian in respect of frequency, site of repair initiation, and the length and syntactic class of the target word[7] in recycling and replacing repairs. Then, in the light of these cross-linguistic examinations, I will consider the potential relationship between the two repair operations by finding connections between the results concerning recycling and the results concerning replacing both in the previous literature and in my investigation. In order to find an explanation for my findings, I extend my research to further same-turn repair operations. As a first step, I select inserting and aborting as the operations to be explored. Finally, I propose the preference hierarchy model of same-turn repair operations, which, I argue, is able to describe same-turn repair operations relative to each other.

The aim of this book is, therefore, to elaborate a model that is based on the assumption that, despite their various functions, different same-turn repair operation types can be examined relative to each other. Although this model looks at repair operations from a new perspective, not only is it consistent with the results of earlier examinations concerning the phenomenon in the domain of conversation analysis, but it also extends our knowledge of same-turn self-repair.

The book is organised as follows. After this introductory chapter, I first provide the metatheoretical background of the research, i.e., introduce the p-model in Chapter 2, then I also provide the object theoretical, conversation analytical background of my work in Chapter 3. In Chapter 4, I describe the corpus and methodology of the study. In Chapter 5, using examples from the previous literature and the Hungarian corpus, I characterise the repair operations under investigation, namely, recycling, replacing, inserting, and aborting. In Chapter 6,

I examine recycling and replacing relative to each other. In Chapter 7, I extend my comparative analysis to inserting and aborting, and propose a preference hierarchy model for same-turn repair operations in talk-in-interaction. In Chapter 8, I summarise the results and conclude my study.

The metatheoretical background of the research: Kertész and Rákosi's (2012, 2014) p-model of plausible argumentation

2.1 The main issues of the model

My object theoretical examination will rely on a nearly five-hour-long Hungarian corpus consisting of 17 Hungarian everyday conversations, but I will take into consideration other data sources as well, such as previous studies by Fox et al. (2009) and Fox et al. (2010) on nine different areally and typologically diverse languages. The integration of these data sources should be done carefully. For this reason, as well as to make the particular steps of my argumentation clearer, I will also give a metatheoretical reflection on my research, for which I will use Kertész and Rákosi's (2012, 2014) p-model of plausible argumentation.

The p-model has been elaborated by Kertész and Rákosi (2012, 2014) in order to solve a central methodological problem in linguistics, namely, what types of data/evidence can be used and how these types of data/evidence work in linguistic theories (Kertész and Rákosi 2012: 1). The model also aims to reveal the relationship between the argumentation structure of theories and the structure and function of data and evidence, a relationship which is close but hidden, according to Kertész and Rákosi (2012: 2). The p-model reflects on, for example, the role of data and evidence in linguistic theorising, what subtypes of data can be regarded as evidence, how different linguistic theories should treat the useable types of data/evidence, or the treatment of problems in linguistic theorising. The most important innovations of the p-model are the following: 1) it works with a new concept of data; 2) it claims that all kinds of linguistic data are uncertain; 3) uncertainty is explicated by the p-model as plausibility; 4) according to the model, linguistic theorising is a dynamic process of plausible argumentation which is cyclic and prismatic in its nature; 5) the p-model regards inconsistency as the natural property of linguistic theories, and offers several techniques to handle it, making problem solving in linguistic theorising more effective; 6) it argues for the pluralism of linguistic theorising, which means that there may be more than one possible solution to a certain problem (Kertész and Rákosi 2014: 5). Since the p-model reflects on linguistic theorising from a metatheoretical point of view in the way described above, applying it in the course of object scientific research makes the results more reliable. In the next three sections, I introduce three of the most important innovations of the model: its concept of plausibility, its notion of the dynamic process of plausible argumentation, and the problem-solving strategies it offers. The p-model says that most of the statements are not true with certainty but only plausible. Since it can differentiate between the degrees of plausibility of statements originating from different sources, using the concept of plausibility during my argumentation will help me in evaluating the set of statements from previous literature and my own argumentation, as well as in deciding between them if necessary. The notion of the dynamic process of plausible argumentation will help me look at my object theoretical argumentation from the outside, with metatheoretically conscious eyes. This will reduce the danger of mistakes in my argumentation. Finally, using the problem-solving strategies the p-model describes, I can solve emerging problems, for example, when I face inconsistency in the set of statements at a certain stage of my argumentation. Using these three metatheoretical concepts consciously during my object theoretical argumentation, the preference hierarchy model that I will obtain as the result of my argumentation process will be more reliable than without a metatheoretical reflection.

2.2 The notion of plausibility: the uncertainty of linguistic data

One of the most important innovations of the p-model is the recognition that linguistic data are most of the time uncertain. The model accounts for this uncertainty with the help of the notion of plausibility and plausible statements. It defines a datum as a statement with a positive plausibility value (strength of acceptability) originating from a direct source (e.g., corpus, linguistic intuition, experiment) (Kertész and Rákosi 2012: 169). A source is regarded as a direct source with respect to a statement, if, on the basis of its reliability, the given statement is assigned a plausibility value. The p-model is able to treat and use uncertain statements by placing them in the argumentation process systematically as follows. In a sense, data (plausible statements) function as starting points for the argumentation process: plausibility values, which they receive directly from direct sources, enter the argumentation process through them. However, they supply the linguistic theory with plausibility values not only in a direct, but also in an indirect way, when functioning as the premises of plausible inferences. Plausible inferences are therefore indirect sources of linguistic theorising because a hypothesis obtained as the conclusion of such an inference receives a plausibility value indirectly, from the datum serving as a premise of the inference. The main body of a given argumentation process is constituted by chains of plausible inferences (Kertész and Rákosi 2012: 169–184; 2014: 37–46).

The p-model differentiates between three types of plausible inferences. The first type consists of cases where the premises are consistent and there is a logical consequence relation between the premises and the conclusion; however, at least one of the premises is not true with certainty[1] but only plausible (deductive inferences). The second group is formed by the instances in which the premises are true with certainty, and they are consistent; nonetheless, the premises and the conclusion are not connected by a logical consequence relation but only by a semantic relation (e.g., analogy, necessary or sufficient condition, causality, etc.). This semantic relation has to be extendable to the so-called latent background assumptions. The latent background assumptions, which have to be plausible, true, or at least not known to be false or implausible according to some source, supplement the set of premises, and from the new set of statements a deductively valid inference can be obtained (Kertész and Rákosi 2012: 99; 2014: 22). It is of great importance in the model that the plausibility of a hypothesis obtained as the conclusion of such an inference is influenced by the plausibility of the latent background assumptions as well. In the case of inductive inferences, for example, the latent background assumption is that the cases not investigated also possess the characteristics of the examined ones. The third type of plausible inferences differs from the second group only in one respect: among the premises of these inferences, there is at least one which is not certainly true but only plausible (Kertész and Rákosi 2012: 56–128; 2014: 20–29).

The p-model's concept of evidence grasps the relationship between hypotheses and data. Evidence in this sense is not an objective, given subcategory of data; any datum can function as evidence for a hypothesis in a given argumentation process if it is a premise of a plausible inference that makes the hypothesis plausible. The notion of evidence in the model is thus interpreted relative to a given hypothesis of a given theory; consequently, it plays a crucial role in the evaluation and comparison of the plausibility of rival hypotheses, i.e., in the problem-solving process (Kertész and Rákosi 2012: 178–184; 2014: 41–46).

2.3 The problem-solving process

2.3.1 The cyclic and prismatic nature of linguistic theorising – plausible argumentation

In order to judge the plausibility value of the premises of an inference, and the semantic relation between the premises and the conclusion, we need all information that may be relevant. For this reason, the p-model has introduced the notion of *p-context*, which includes a set of sources on the basis of which the plausibility value of statements can be judged. It also includes a set of statements with their plausibility values assigned to them with respect to the sources mentioned, as well as with their logical and semantic structure. Finally, the accepted methodological norms also belong to the p-context (Kertész and Rákosi 2012: 122; 2014: 27). The p-context can be informationally overdetermined if both a statement and its negation are made plausible by some (different) source. In these cases, the p-context is *p-inconsistent*. The p-context can also be informationally underdetermined if it contains statements neither plausible nor implausible with respect to any source within it. This is a case of *p-incompleteness*. P-inconsistency and p-incompleteness are called *p-problems* in the p-model (Kertész and Rákosi 2012: 130–134; 2014: 29–32). In order to solve a p-problem, the p-context has to be re-evaluated. The process which transforms a p-problematic p-context into another p-context which is not (or is less) p-problematic, is the systematic and heuristic process of plausible argumentation. As the re-evaluation of the p-problematic p-context may often raise new problems, it usually does not lead immediately to an unproblematic p-context. The argumentation process is therefore not linear but *cyclic*: we return to problems again and again and re-evaluate our previous decisions, for example, about the rejection or acceptance of statements. Since the cycles always change the perspective from which the p-context is evaluated, the argumentation process is not only cyclic, but also *prismatic*. An argumentation cycle consists of the following phases: 1) the *extension* of the p-context by new sources, methods, and statements; 2) the *coordination* of the extended p-context (e.g., checking the consistency of the set of statements, comparing the plausibility values of statements originating from the old and the new sources, comparing the old and the new pieces of information concerning the reliability of the sources, etc.); 3) the *modification* of the extended and coordinated p-context, i.e., working out the p-context which will be the revised version of the starting p-context; and 4) the *comparison* of the rival solutions (Kertész and Rákosi 2012: 134–153; 2014: 32–34).

2.3.2 Problem-solving strategies

As was noted in the previous section, the p-context can be informationally overdetermined if both a statement and its negation are plausible to a certain extent at some stage of the argumentation process. The p-model considers such inconsistencies to be the natural property of linguistic theories. It offers effective problem-solving strategies, all of which involve the retrospective re-evaluation of the p-context (i.e., the previously accepted data, data sources, evidence, plausibility values, and methodological norms) from different perspectives (Kertész and Rákosi 2012: 134–153; 2014: 32–34; see the previous section). The *Contrastive Strategy* compares contradictory statements and regards them as rival alternatives. By applying the Contrastive Strategy, we aim to reach a decision between the rival alternatives on the basis of the information available. The continuation of the Contrastive Strategy may be either the *Exclusive Strategy* or the *Combinative Strategy*. While the Exclusive Strategy makes a decision between the rival alternatives, the Combinative Strategy keeps both: it elaborates and separates two unproblematic p-context versions which will make up the whole p-context. These different p-context versions are regarded as co-existing alternatives. The reason for this can be that the two versions illuminate a certain phenomenon from different but equally important perspectives. The p-model always leaves open the possibility of more alternative solutions and further argumentation cycles (on problem-solving strategies, see Kertész and Rákosi 2012: 153–161; 2014: 35–37).

As I have argued earlier, building the metatheoretical issues explicated above into my object theoretical discussion will help me consider my argumentation from 'the outside', i.e., with meta-conscious eyes, and thus will reduce the danger of making a logical or any other error during my argumentation. I start my object theoretical discussion with the introduction of the object theoretical background of my research, namely, conversation analysis.

CHAPTER 3

The object theoretical background of the research: conversation analysis

3.1 Talk-in-interaction

Conversation analysis is an approach to language use and social interaction which assumes the orderliness of these phenomena and aims to investigate their over-all structure (Stivers and Sidnell 2013: 2). According to this approach, as Sacks, Schegloff, and Jefferson (1974: 700) point out in their classic article, conversation is a vehicle for interaction between speakers who have any potential identities and any potential familiarity. That is to say, language is a vehicle for social action (Stivers and Sidnell 2013: 3). Talk-in-interaction in this sense is *acting*: it takes place in sequences of *turns* (a speaker's contribution to the talk at a time)[1] in each of which we *act*; we design each turn to do something which is contingent on the prior turn, and by doing this we also set up contingencies for what comes next (Drew 2013: 131). Levinson (2013) regards action as a *main job* assigned to the turn. His definition of what counts as a main job focuses on the sequential environment of the turn: a main job is what the response has to deal with so as to count as an adequate subsequent turn (Levinson 2013: 107). A turn can therefore perform more than one action, more than one main job at a time. However, we should differentiate between actions and off-record doings (Levinson 2013), when, for example, an answer to a question at the same time hints that the questioner should have known the answer already (Stivers 2011). It is difficult to respond to these less official doings directly in such a way that we do not completely redirect the conversation (Levinson 2013: 107), and hence they do not count as action. Schegloff (2007: 8) differentiates between the action-concept of speech act theory (Austin 1962, 1979; Searle 1969, 1975, 1976; Searle and Vanderveken 1985) and conversation analysis. While the former defines classes or categories of action and tries to identify their conceptual components (e.g., what makes an action a promise), the latter begins with the particular instances in their embedding contexts, i.e., it tries to identify what a certain bit of talk is designed to do. According to Schegloff, this strategy can lead the analyst to discover new actions which do not have vernacular names, and which speech act theory could not analyse (Schegloff 2007: 8). Moreover, it can also happen that in a particular situation the interactants understand something different by an action than what is usually understood by it (Schegloff 2007: 9). In this way, the number of possible actions in our conversations is unknown (see the action of *problem-raising* in Example (13) below) (Schegloff 2007: xiv).

The concept *turn-constructional unit* (TCU) was established by Sacks et al. (1974: 702) as the turn-constructional component. TCUs are the building blocks of turns (Schegloff 2007: 3). The criterial feature of a TCU is that it has to realise a recognisable action in the context (Schegloff 2007: 4). A TCU thus has to realise at least one action, but it may embody more than one action as well (Schegloff 2007: 9); in other words, it is possible for a TCU to implement more than one main job at a time. For example, an action can serve as the vehicle for carrying out another action (Schegloff 2007: 9): questioning can be the vehicle by which making a request is implemented (e.g., *Can you open the door?*). Since an adequate next turn could deal with both the questioning and the request, both actions are implemented by the TCU.[2] If a speaker starts a turn, s/he has the right and obligation to produce one TCU (Schegloff 2007: 9). Approaching the possible completion of the first TCU, transition to the next speaker becomes relevant, but it is also possible for the speaker to extend the same TCU or start another TCU without transition. The next occurrence of a possible TCU completion is equivalent to the next *transition-relevance place* (Sacks et al. 1974: 704; Schegloff 2007: 4). In Example (13), Cili and Anna talk about Christmas. Anna is raising the question of when it is appropriate to celebrate Christmas together for a couple who have been going out with each other for some time.

(13) (bea003n001)

```
01   C:   bővül      a       család    még      jobban.
          grows      the     family    even     more
          'the family becomes even bigger.

          (0.3)

02   A:   hát        igen.   de     ez     is     olyan   nehéz      hogy     igazából
          well[2]    yes     but    this   also   so      difficult  that     actually
          well, yes. but it is also so difficult that
```

03   *amikor   már   valaki: hosszabb   ideje   együtt*
    when   already   somebody   longer   time   together
    when actually you: have been going out with somebody for a longer time

04   *van   valakivel   hogy   hogy   mikor   jön*
    is   somebody.COM   that   that   when   comes
    that that when does

05   *az   a   el   az   a   pont   amikor   már*
    that   the   PVB   that   the   point   when   already
    the time come

06   *együtt   is   karácsonyoz* [*nak   mer*]   *.hh azér* =
    together   also   celebrate.Christmas.3PL.INDEF   because   that.CAU
    to celebrate also Christmas toge[ther because] .hh for that matter =

07   C: [mhm   ]

08   A: =   *egy   darabig   még   mindig   mindenki   vissz-   a*
    a   period.TERM   still   always   everybody   ba-⁴   the
    =   still for a while everybody ba- with her/his

09   [*saját csa*]*ládjával*   *otthon   és   akkor   maximum   másnap*=
    own   family.POSS.3SG.COM   at.home   and   then   at.the.most   next.day
    [own fa   ]mily at home and then they meet next day at the most =

10   C: [*ottho:n*]
    at.home
    [at ho:me]

11   A: = *találkoznak   de   (.)   nem   tudom.   ezt   én*
    meet.3PL.INDEF   but   not   know.1SG.DEF   this.ACC   I
    = but (.) I don't know I can't

12   *még   így   nem   tudom   elképzelni   de   majd*
    yet   in.this.way   not   can.1SG.DEF   imagine.INF   but   sometime
    imagine it in this way yet but sometime

13   *biztos   hogyha   má   ilyen   saját   közös   kuckó*
    certainly   if   already   such   own   joint   nook
    certainly if we already have our own joint nook

14   *lesz   ak* [*kor   már*] *úgy   de   (.)   furi* =
    will.be   then   already   in.that.way   but   strange
    then [it will be] in that way but (.) it will still be strange. =

15   C: [mhm   ]

```
16   A:  =   lesz      azér.  nálatok        hogy   van,   Cili?
                 will.be   still   at.your.place   how    is     Cili
         =   what about you, Cili?

17       ((laughing))      mer      te    már
                           because   you   already
         ((laughing)) 'cause you have already

18       [férjnél          vagy. ]
         husband.ADE   are
         [   got married.    ]

19   C:  [  hát    mi ]        is      sokáig
            well   we                  also    for.a.long.time
         [  well,  we ]   also for a long time
```

C: the family becomes even bigger.
      (0.3)
A: well yes. but it is also so difficult that when actually you: have been going out with
      somebody for a longer time that that when does the time come to celebrate also
      Christmas toge   [ther because] .hh for that matter still for a while everybody =
C: [m h m   ]
A: = ba- with her/his   [own fa   ]mily at home and =
C: [at ho:me]
A: = then they meet next day at the most but (.) I don't know I can't imagine it in this
      way yet but sometime certainly if we already have our own joint nook then
      [it will be] in that way but (.) still it will be strange. what about you, Cili? =
C: [m h m]
A: = ((laughing)) 'cause you have already   [got married.]
C: [well, we] also for a long time...

In line 01, a telling is being accomplished by Cili (cf. Schegloff 2007: 7). In line 02,
Anna's response *hát igen* 'well yes' constitutes the first TCU of her turn. The second unit which a potential response as an adequate next turn could deal with, i.e.,
the next action in Anna's turn, is a *problem-raising*. In lines 02–16, she raises the
question of when a couple should decide to celebrate Christmas together. This action is implemented by a TCU which Anna extends twice: first she describes how
couples usually spend Christmas before celebrating together (lines 06–11), then
she illustrates the difficulty of the question with her own personal experience
(lines 11–16) (on the possibilities of turn-extension in Hungarian, see Németh
2007–2008). In lines 16–18, Anna asks Cili how she and her husband have solved
the problem. This is the last TCU (and the last action) in Anna's turn, which she
also extends. In the extension she gives her reason for selecting Cili as the next
speaker: Cili has already got married.

Apart from action formation (Levinson 2013) and TCUs (Clayman 2013), there are various fundamental structures in conversation, such as turn design (Drew 2013), sequence organisation (Stivers 2013), preference (Pomerantz and Heritage 2013), or repair (Kitzinger 2013). In this book, I aim to focus on the organisation of repair; nevertheless, as all the structures listed above are related to one another, I must examine repair by taking into consideration the other structures as well.

3.2 The organisation of conversational repair: What constitutes the domain of repair operation in conversation analysis?

Since the classic article by Schegloff and his colleagues (1977: 361), who pointed out that an organisation of repair works in conversation to deal with recurrent problems in speaking, hearing, and understanding, repair has become one of the central fields of conversation analytic research. Its domain is 'the set of practices whereby a co-interactant interrupts the ongoing course of action to attend to possible trouble in speaking, hearing or understanding the talk' (Kitzinger 2013: 229). This means that in the conversation analytic framework, repair involves only the problem-treating practices which suspend the progressivity of the ongoing turn or sequence, and thus the ongoing activity. According to Schegloff (2007: xiv), the general motive of repair is to ensure that the interaction does not freeze where it is when a problem emerges, to maintain or restore intersubjectivity, and to make the turn, the sequence, and the activity progress to possible completion. In other words, paradoxically, repair involves the temporary interruption of the ongoing activity so as to maintain its progression to possible completion. The maintenance of the ongoing activity is possible only if there is a world which the co-interactants know and hold in common. This common world is grasped by the notion of *intersubjectivity* (Schegloff 1992: 1296). As Schegloff (1992: 1299) points out, the restoration and maintenance of intersubjectivity is built into the procedural infrastructure of talk-in-interaction involving the self-righting mechanism of the organisation of repair. Repair is therefore a means by which intersubjectivity is maintained and defended in talk-in-interaction (Schegloff 1992: 1338). This explains what the term *trouble* means in the definition of repair: trouble involves everything which may endanger the maintenance of intersubjectivity, and repair is initiated when the speaker cannot handle this kind of problem without interrupting the ongoing course of action.

After differentiating between self- and other-initiated repair (see Chapter 1), Kitzinger (2013: 231) emphasises that both types of repair interrupt the progressivity of the interaction, but while same-turn self-repair suspends the progressivity of the turn, other-repair suspends the progressivity of the sequence. As far as the technology of the two types of repair is concerned, the initiation of other-repair can occur in a range of formats which vary along a continuum. The ordering principle of this continuum is how precisely the format grasps the trouble-source. While the open class repair initiator form (e.g., *Huh? Pardon?*) does not grasp the repairable precisely and thus counts as the weakest repair initiator form, offering a candidate understanding is the resaying of the trouble-source in other words and therefore is the strongest repair initiator format (Schegloff et al. 1977: 367–368; Kitzinger 2013: 249). While Example (14) shows an open class repair initiator form, in Example (15) other-repair is initiated by offering a candidate understanding. While offering a candidate understanding of the referent of *Bullocks*, Stan carries out a self-repair as well, a word search for the name of the Plaza theatre (see Example (8) in Section 1.1).

(14) (Kitzinger 2013: 232)

```
1   Clt:   .hhhhh But it nourished him (.) in utero
2          well did it.
3          (.)
4   Ang:   Pardon?
5   Clt:   It nour- The placenta nourished him
6          .hhh in utero
7   Ang:   Yeah
```

(15) (Schegloff 2013: 49)

```
01  Joy:   Why don'tchoo: go into Westwoo:d, (0.4) and go to
02         Bullocks.
03         (1.2)
04  Stn:   Bullocks? ya mean that one right u:m (1.1) tch! (.)
05         right by thee: u:m (.) whazit the Plaza? theatre::=
06  Joy:   = Uh huh,
```

Regarding self-repair, the interruption of the turn-in-progress may be achieved by a cut-off or devices such as *um, uh* (*ö* in Hungarian) or sound stretches. It is crucial to note that, instead of ipso facto initiating repair, these forms only alert the recipient to the possibility of repair. Conversely, initiating repair can also occur tacitly without any explicit indication (Kitzinger 2013: 239). In Example (16), Anna is describing what her family usually eats during the Christmas holidays.

(16) (bea003n001: 171)

```
01  A:  mi    is     eszünk            mondjuk   év      közben
        we    also   eat.1PL.INDEF     anyway    year    during
        'anyway, we also eat (lentils) during the year
```

02   *is   de   szi-   ö: ö   január   elsején*
      also   but   New-   u:h uh   January   first.POSS.3SG.SUP
      but on **New- u:h uh on the first of January**

03   *mindig   lencsét   eszünk.*
      always   lentil.ACC   eat.1PL.INDEF
      we always eat lentils.'

In line 02, Anna interrupts the ongoing TCU by cutting off the segment she is in the course of producing (*szi-*). After two *öö*-s, she produces the time adverb *január elsején* 'on the first of January'. Since *szilveszter* means 'New Year's Eve' in Hungarian, and the first of January is the day after New Year's Eve, the word Anna interrupts is likely to be *szilveszter*, which she replaces with *január elsején* 'on the first of January'. In this repair operation, the cut-off is a repair-initiating technique that Anna uses to initiate a replacing repair.

In Example (17), the repair initiation happens tacitly. Donna retrospectively inserts *complaints* before *procedure* and in this way specifies the kind of procedure she is speaking about. With this repair operation she restricts the category of referents.

(17) (Wilkinson and Weatherall 2011: 68)

Don: you know th' procedure **complaints procedure** goes
        out the window the minute you take legal action.

Schegloff et al. (1977: 363) refer to self-initiated and other-initiated repair as covering a more general domain of occurrences, while self- and other-correction are particular subtypes in this domain. The point in this distinction is that the term *correction* is usually understood as the replacing of an error by what is correct, whereas the phenomena Schegloff and his colleagues address are not limited to such cases. For example, a word search is in the repair domain but does not count as correction. Let us see the word search in Example (8) again, repeated here as Example (18), from another perspective. Here we cannot see any mistakes that need to be fixed; however, there is still a problem that prevents the ongoing turn from progressing towards possible completion: Stan cannot immediately produce the next relevant word and employs several time-gaining devices to delay its production (e.g., elongated *ums* and pauses).

(18) (Schegloff 2013: 49)

Joy: Why don'tchoo: go into Westwoo:d, (0.4) and go to
        Bullocks.
        (1.2)

Stn: Bullocks? ya mean that one **right u:m (1.1) tch! (.)**
       right by thee: u:m (.) whazit the Plaza? theatre::=
Joy: =Uh huh,

Repair can also be initiated without an apparent error, and nothing is excludable from the class *repairable* (Schegloff et al. 1977: 363). According to Schegloff (2013: 47), repairing is often merely altering. In these cases, we cannot identify a problem to be fixed, but the turn can be better realised by an alteration (see Example (17)). Conversely, an audible error does not always yield repair or correction. In Example (19), the Avon Lady produces *gery* instead of *very*, but she does not correct herself.

(19) (Schegloff et al. 1977: 363)

Avon Lady: And for ninety-nine cents uh especially in,
             Rapture, and the Au Coeur which is the newest
             fragrances, uh that is a **gery** good value.
Customer: Uh huh,

Finally, it can also happen that efforts at repair (as well as correction) fail. For this reason, the initiation of reparative segments and their completion (i.e., the solution of the problem) should be distinguished (Schegloff et al. 1977: 364). The term *repair* refers to the success of the repair procedure (Schegloff et al. 1977: 363). In Example (20), instead of producing the completion of the TCU, the speaker expresses anger.

(20) (Schegloff et al. 1977: 364).

C: C'n you tell me (1.0) D'you have any records of whether you whether you
     who you sent- Oh(hh) shit.

The most common type of repair is self-repair in the TCU containing the repairable (see Examples (16), (17), and (18)). In this type of self-repair, the speaker of the trouble-source initiates repair, i.e., interrupts the progressivity of the turn to attend to the trouble-source and produces a repair solution before the TCU comes to a possible completion. The frequency of this repair type can partly be explained by the observation that the speaker of the trouble-source has the first opportunity to initiate repair because of the turn-taking system (Sacks et al. 1974; Kitzinger 2013: 232; Section 3.1).

In the framework of conversation analysis, the concept of *repair operation* is not defined explicitly. This is perhaps because, according to the conversation analytic viewpoint, it is the analysis that 'is responsible for the determination of what will constitute a "case" or an "instance" of a putative phenomenon' (Schegloff 2009: 391). And, in the course of such an examination, 'the researcher's understanding of what the phenomenon is' can be transformed by 'each candidate instance' of this 'putative phenomenon' (Schegloff 2009: 391). However, when a researcher sits down to do this kind of analysis, and looks at the recorded material, s/he needs to know first what to select as a *candidate instance of a putative phenomenon*. Without a previous understanding of what a putative phenomenon can be, we cannot select our candidate instances. Therefore, selecting what to analyse requires a previous determination of the domain of our putative phenomena. If we take a closer look at the other statement, which says that during an analysis, 'each candidate instance of a putative phenomenon' can 'transform the researcher's understanding of what the phenomenon is' (Schegloff 2009: 391), we will realise that it is accompanied by a presupposition (cf. Kiefer 1982): if something can be transformed, then it already has to exist before the transformation. This means that before the analysis the researcher already has to have an understanding of what that putative phenomenon is. If that were not the case, we could not read about any groups of phenomena in the conversation analytic literature, such as repair, self-repair, repair operation, or the ten main same-turn repair operations (see Chapter 1). Even in corpus-based research, we constantly decide which occurrences to select as instances of a particular phenomenon, relying on our knowledge of what characteristics make something, for example, a repair, and then, using our intuition, we identify these characteristics in our corpus. Consequently, the source and the nature of our statements in a corpus-based study is complex: the theoretical framework that is used by the researcher and the researcher's intuition cannot be eliminated (cf. Nagy C., Németh T., and Németh 2018).

In this section, I collect some statements containing the terms *repair operation* and *repair* in the conversation analytic literature, and try to make explicit what is meant by the term *repair operation* and how it is related to the domain of repair. In doing this, I rely on the p-model explicated in Chapter 2 (Kertész and Rákosi 2012, 2014). With the help of the p-model, I try to uncover the latent background assumptions concerning the notion of repair operation and its relationship with the domain of repair. These background assumptions do not appear explicitly but lie behind the statements. Supplying our set of statements with them, we obtain new statements as the conclusions of plausible inferences. These new statements already contain explicit information about what a repair operation is and how it is related to the phenomenon of repair.

Statement 1:   The domain of repair is 'the set of practices whereby a co-interactant interrupts the ongoing course of action to attend to possible trouble in speaking, hearing or understanding the talk' (Kitzinger 2013: 229).

Statement 2:   'Speakers employ' same-turn repair operations 'to deal with some putative trouble-source in an ongoing turn-at-talk in conversation or to alter it in some interactionally consequential way' (Schegloff 2013: 43).

We can intuitively accept that *dealing* with some putative trouble-source or *altering* it in some interactionally consequential way belong to the category of *attending* to possible trouble in talk-in-interaction. In this case, as the conclusion of a plausible inference from Statement 1 and Statement 2, Statement 3 presents itself (see Kertész and Rákosi 2012: 56ff.; 2014: 20ff.; Section 2.2).

Statement 3:   Repair operations are employed in the domain of repair.

Let us see some other statements. Schegloff introduces his study *Ten operations in self-initiated, same-turn repair* already quoted above, in the following way:

Statement 4:   'this installment is addressed to a sharply demarcated, albeit substantial, domain, and one facet of the repair undertaken there. The domain is "self-initiated, same-turn repair"; the facet is the sorts of operations that get implemented there' (Schegloff 2013: 41).

Implication of Statement 4:   Same-turn repair operations get implemented in the domain of self-initiated, same-turn repair.

From the implication of Statement 4, Statement 5 follows.

Statement 5:   Repair operations get implemented in the domain of repair.

In the same place, Schegloff writes the following:

Statement 6:   'within the self-imposed domain to be treated here, only the repair *operations* are to be taken up, and not other facets of these repairs, such as the *components* of the repair segments through which the operations are prosecuted' (Schegloff 2013: 41, italics original).

Implication of Statement 6:   Repair operations are prosecuted through the components of the repair segments.

Statement 7:   According to the *Oxford Advanced Learner's Dictionary of Current English,* the verb *prosecute* means 'to continue taking part in or doing sth' (Wehmeier 2000: 1017).

Statement 8:   'Repair is not composed of repair operations but rather implements them' (anonymous reviewer of *Research on Language and Social Interaction*)

Statement 9:   'the operation the repair is accomplishing (anonymous reviewer of *Research on Language and Social Interaction*)

Statement 10:   'The repair operation – that is, the interactional move that is performed by the speaker' (Egbert, Golato, and Robinson 2009: 104).

Statement 11:   'Instead of the conventional use of nouns like "replacement", "insertion", and the like, I have opted for action terms like "replacing", "inserting" and the like to emphasise that these are *operations* that speakers carry through – that they *do*, not pre-packaged products that they select' (Schegloff 2013: 43, italics original).

All these statements refer to the concept of repair operation as an interactional move, as an action: repair operations are employed, get implemented, prosecuted, or accomplished according to the above sources. But how is the concept of repair operation related to the concept of repair? Based on Statements 6–9, we can say that repair operations are prosecuted through the components of the repair segments.

Therefore, taking into consideration all the above statements, in this book I will regard repair operation as *the action being accomplished by the speaker through the repair segment*. As I pointed out in the Introduction, the main purpose of my research is to find an answer to the question of whether it is possible to analyse and interpret same-turn repair operations relative to each other. Before beginning this search, it is necessary to describe the corpus and methodology of the study.

CHAPTER 4

The corpus and methodology of the study

The findings of the research presented in this book are based on two corpora consisting of everyday Hungarian conversations (of 38 speakers across 17 interactions). One corpus consists of nine approximately 20-minute-long conversations recorded at the Institute of Psychology, University of Szeged (SZTEPSZI corpus),[1] and the other consists of eight approximately 15-minute-long conversations recorded at the Kempelen Farkas Speech Research Laboratory at the Research Institute for Linguistics of the Hungarian Academy of Sciences, Budapest (Hungarian speech database, BEA; Gósy 2012).[2] The extracts from the corpora are marked as SZTEPSZI1, SZTEPSZI2, etc. and bea001, bea002, etc., respectively. The total length of the recordings constituting the conversations in the corpus is 4 hours 58 minutes 42 seconds. The participants (three in each conversation) were adults of varying ages. While the SZTEPSZI corpus consists of video recordings, the conversations from the BEA database are audio recorded. The participants were talking in an acoustically controlled room in order to achieve the best-possible sound quality. The subjects were not instructed or controlled in any way. In order to help them start talking, in the SZTEPSZI conversations there were some pieces of paper naming topics on the table around which they sat. However, the participants were not required to use these topics, but encouraged to talk about anything they were interested in. Similarly, the conversations from the BEA speech database were initiated by one of the participants asking a question (e.g., *How did you spend Christmas? What is your opinion about getting a driving licence in Hungary?* etc.), which shaped the course of the interaction to a certain extent, but the participants could equally contribute to the conversations in each case.[3]

Although the initial object theoretical framework of this study is conversation analysis, my research aims established in Chapter 1 make it necessary to diverge from the 'conversation analytic mentality' (Schenkein 1978) in some respects.

First, the metatheoretical framework of my examination, i.e., the p-model of plausible argumentation, regards data as statements with positive plausibility values (strength of acceptability) originating from direct sources (e.g., corpus, linguistic intuition, experiment) (see Section 2.2). As I have mentioned in the Introduction, I will use the term *data* in the sense of the p-model, and in all other sections I avoid using it in the conversation analytic sense. For this reason, I will refer to the recordings I have analysed by the term *corpus*.

Second, Stivers and Sidnell (2013: 2) emphasise that the conversation analytic method is primarily qualitative. It describes and explains the structures of social interaction relying on a case-by-case analysis, which leads to generalisations across cases but prevents them from congealing into an aggregate. This means that conversation analysis allows for quantitative analysis to a certain extent (seeking to notice patterns and distributional regularities), but this quantitative analysis only provides reassurance that a given phenomenon is not an isolated usage of some local setting (a particular speaker or category of speakers) but has 'a prima facie robustness' (Schegloff 2009: 389). According to Schegloff (2009: 389), statistical methods force the research to shift from the empirical analysis of the individual cases to 'puzzling' analyses on larger corpuses, which makes the cases congeal into an aggregate, and for this reason they do not fit into the conversation analytic mentality. This suggests that the conversation analytic framework regards quantitative analysis as searching for regularities and making generalisations, and statistical analysis as doing the same things on a larger corpus. Schegloff (1993) also argues against conducting statistical analyses when asking whether the sample of data analysed in this way can provide reliable findings on the larger universe from which it was drawn. This reasoning, however, also questions the reliability of the inductive analyses which conversation analysis prefers, because the generalisations conversation analysis allows for (e.g., on the preference for self-correction as opposed to other-correction) work in a similar way. Furthermore, according to Schegloff (2009: 389), the quantitative analysis in conversation analysis always leads back to the individual cases when, for example, the researcher specifies a phenomenon and shows its variants or encounters a problem which makes her/him reanalyse the particular instances. Schegloff says that, when conducting statistical analyses, the researcher codes the recordings, which results in the distribution of the particular instances according to pre-selected variables (2009: 390). Instead of making the examination responsive to the observable features of the particular cases explored one-by-one, coding is a prescribed inquiry during which the variables cannot be determined or modified (2009: 390–391).

In contrast to this reasoning, I argue that it is impossible to analyse recordings and make observations without any preliminary theoretical considerations. In

Lehmann's (2004) view, any statements made by the researcher regarding a linguistic phenomenon are based on abstraction and semiotic processes; in other words, they are not given at the outset but are, at least to some extent, produced by the researcher. Kertész and Rákosi (2012: 242) emphasise that the conceptual apparatus of a given theory is closely related to the methods and methodological principles of any examinations carried out in the framework of this theory and determines the level of abstraction at which the investigated phenomena can be captured. The aspects of the phenomena which we can grasp and the ways we can describe these aspects are also determined by the conceptual apparatus used during the investigation (Kertész and Rákosi 2012: 243). That is to say, the theoretical framework within which the researcher works cannot be eliminated even when s/he analyses speech events recorded in their original form. For example, selecting occurrences and labelling them as examples of the phenomenon of replacing, recycling, inserting, etc. must occur on the basis of pre-selected variables, i.e., the variables whose values make a phenomenon repair, self-repair, and recycling, replacing, inserting, aborting, etc. These variables are determined by the conceptual apparatus of conversation analysis. For example, an occurrence belongs to the phenomenon of repair only if it interrupts the ongoing course of action: it is not labelled a repair phenomenon if it does not interrupt the ongoing course of action. In other words, any kind of categorisation requires a conceptual apparatus which determines the features a putative phenomenon should possess in order to belong to a certain group of phenomena. The point is that the coding process, which results in the distribution of instances according to pre-selected variables (Schegloff 2009: 390), even in conventional statistical analyses, does not exclude the kind of analysis CA prefers. What is more, in order to be reliable, it should be based on a careful examination of the candidate phenomena on a case-by-case basis which 'treats each case in its particulars' (Schegloff 2009: 391) and is sensitive to the sequential environment of interactional items (ten Have 1990). If we search for regularities and make generalisations on a group of cases, each of which has been analysed previously in a qualitative way (as conversation analysis does) or by including more cases (as statistical analysis does), the only thing that changes is that our generalisations will be more reliable. In other words, empirical generalisations can become stronger if we conduct statistical analyses on the same set of cases. Consequently, not only is it the case that qualitative and statistical methods in the same research are not mutually exclusive, but they are mutually reinforcing. This has also been recognised by Fox and her colleagues (2009, 2010) when they conducted statistical analyses in their cross-linguistic research on same-turn self-repair in the framework of conversation analysis. Relying on these considerations, during my investigation I will also use both qualitative and statistical methods.

While Chapter 5 introduces the repair operations investigated in the study by analysing examples, Chapters 6 and 7 present two successive phases of the research. The first phase is carried out using eight conversations from the BEA database and two conversations from the SZTEPSZI corpus (17 speakers across ten interactions, total length: 2 hours 25 minutes 4 seconds). Since the results of this study provide a motivation for the continuation of the research on an extended corpus, the second phase is carried out using eight conversations from the BEA database and nine conversations from the SZTEPSZI corpus (38 speakers across 17 interactions, total length: 4 hours 58 minutes 42 seconds).

In Chapter 6, I examine recycling and replacing relative to each other. First, I extend the cross-linguistic investigation of Fox et al. (2009) and Fox et al. (2010) to Hungarian and try to reveal whether the Hungarian language fits the patterns suggested as universal. Then, in the light of these cross-linguistic examinations, I will consider the potential relationship between the two repair operations by finding connections between the results concerning recycling and the results concerning replacing, both in the previous literature and in my investigation.

In the first phase of this research, I will examine 1) the frequency of recycling and replacing repairs in the Hungarian corpus, 2) the syntactic category and length of the target word in all recycling and replacing instances, and 3) the location where speakers initiate repair in the target word in all recycling and replacing repairs in the Hungarian corpus. In order to see the relationship between the variables listed above, I will use 2×2 and 2×3 Pearson's chi-square statistics, and calculate the Cramér's V measure of nominal association as well.[4] I first attempt to find out whether the speakers tend to initiate recycling and replacing in monosyllabic, bisyllabic, or multisyllabic,[5] and function or content words, respectively. Labelling function and content words as syntactic classes, I follow Fox et al. (2009). While content words are open-class words with a lexical, statable meaning, the class of function words is closed and carries a grammatical meaning. The reason why they are called syntactic classes is the fact that distinguishing them plays an important role in characterising the syntactic properties of sentences (Selkirk 2008: 464). When I decide whether a particular word in the Hungarian corpus is a function or a content word, I rely on Kenesei (2000). The category of function words consists of closed word classes, which are invariable in a given language state. Their number cannot be increased, neither by borrowing words nor by internal lexical processes. For example, conjunctions, auxiliaries, and articles are function words (Kenesei 2000: 95). Conversely, the category of content words consists of open word classes (e.g., nouns, verbs, and adverbs), the elements of which can be increased without limit by, for example, borrowing words from other languages, derivation, or compounding (Kenesei 2000: 95).

I also try to reveal whether the type of the repair operation, the length of the target word, and/or the syntactic class of the target word influence the site of repair initiation. Considering repair initiation, Schegloff (1979) points out that the most common location of repair initiation is just after the start of a TCU (post-initiation) or just before its completion (pre-completion), for example, in the case of a word after its first sound or just before its last sound (Schegloff 1979: 275). The relevant domain for the post-initiation of a unit (or as Fox et al. (2009) term it, post-beginning) starts after the first sound is recognisable and continues until the first sound is complete, whereas the relevant domain for pre-completion begins just before the final sound is articulated and continues until just before the final sound is complete (Fox et al. 2009: 65). Fox et al. (2009) introduce the term *recognisable completion*. Repair initiation at or after recognisable completion refers to initiations in or after the last sound of the word, while repair initiation before recognisable completion means that the speaker initiates repair before the articulation of the last sound begins (Fox et al. 2009: 71). It is of great importance to note here that the term recognisable completion does not refer to the recognition of the word in which the speaker initiates repair, but to the recognition of the word as completed. While the listener may recognise the word long before it is recognisably completed, recognisable completion allows her/him to assume that the word is finished.

After carrying out these examinations, I take into consideration the results of Fox et al. (2009), Fox et al. (2010), as well as the Hungarian findings, and make a cross-linguistic comparison of recycling and replacing. Finding connections between the results concerning recycling and the results concerning replacing both in the previous literature and in my investigation, I propose a preference hierarchy among recycling initiated after recognisable completion, recycling initiated before recognisable completion, and replacing.

The findings of Chapter 6 motivate the second phase of my study. Searching for an explanation as to why speakers seem to prefer recycling to replacing cross-linguistically, I extend my research to two other same-turn repair operations, namely, inserting and aborting. In Chapter 7, I propose a model which describes repair operations relative to each other. I propose this model on the basis of data from previous research, and the qualitative analysis of examples from the Hungarian corpus (during which I also use statements from previous research), and I also use my intuition when setting up the model and examining its consequences on actions where speakers use more than one repair operation one after the other.

The purpose of the integration of the various sources and methods described above is to enhance the reliability of the hypotheses obtained as the results of my study (cf. Kertész and Rákosi 2014: 221). This is in accordance with Kertész and Rákosi's (2012: 239) metatheoretical finding, namely, that supporting the hypotheses of a given theory by as many types of data (i.e., plausible statements originating from direct sources) and as many sources as possible can increase the plausibility of these hypotheses. This means that the conscious integration of data from various data sources can reduce the uncertainty which may result from the application of a single data source.

Since the purpose of my study is to compare different repair operations with each other, and find a basis for this comparative examination, I have selected four different repair operations to examine first. In the next chapter, using examples from both the Hungarian corpus and earlier studies on other languages, I will introduce these four operations, namely, replacing, recycling, inserting, and aborting. I will illustrate them with several examples from the Hungarian corpus that also appear and are analysed in Németh 2017 from the perspective of their roles in interaction.

CHAPTER 5

Four repair operations

5.1 Replacing

Replacing involves 'a speaker's substituting for a wholly or partially articulated element of a TCU-in-progress another, different[1] element, while retaining the sense that "this is the same utterance"' (Schegloff 2013: 43), i.e., without aborting the ongoing TCU. In Example (21), Ica describes her years spent in a drama group ('one' in line 01 refers to the group). In line 03, she interrupts the ongoing action without aborting it.

(21) (SZTEPSZI1: 661)

```
01  I:  aztán     találtam              egyet,      ((swallow))  az    tök[2]   jó
        then      found.1SG.INDEF       one.ACC                  that  very     good
        'then I found one, ((swallow)) that was very good=
```

```
02      volt      =      csak   .h    így               <feltűnt,
        was.3SG          only         in.this.way       appeared
        =however .h in this way <it appeared to me
```

```
03      hogy      így>           (.)    hát   mennyi?       hány          évet
        that      in.this.way           well[3]  how.many    how.many      year.ACC
        that in this way> (.) well how many? how many years
```

```
04      voltam              ott?       asszem    négyet?       vagy    ötö:t?
        was.1SG.INDEF       there      I.think   four.ACC      or      five.ACC
        did I spend there? I think four? or five?
```

```
05      .h  és       feltűnt       hogy   így-            <minden      évbe:,>
            and      appeared      that   in.this.way     every        year.INE
        .h and it appeared to me that in this way- <every yea:r, >
```

<pre>
06   ugyanazt   tanuljuk.
      same.ACC   learn.1PL.DEF
      we learn the same things.'
</pre>

I: then I found one, ((swallow)) that was very good=however .h in this way <it appeared to me that in this way> (.) well **how many? how many** years did I spend there? I think four? or five? .h and it appeared to me that in this way- <every yea:r, > we learn the same things.

In line 03, Ica replaces the question word *mennyi* 'how many, how much' with the question word *hány* 'how many'. In Hungarian, one can ask questions for countable nouns both with *mennyi* and *hány* (e.g., *Hány almád van? Mennyi almád van?* 'How many apples do you have?'). Asking questions for uncountable nouns, however, is only possible with *mennyi* 'how many, how much' (cf. Lipták 2005: 170). For example, when Hungarian speakers use the word *idő* 'time' as an uncountable noun, the only possible question word they can use is *mennyi* 'how many, how much' (*Mennyi időnk van?* 'How much time do we have?'). Therefore, the countable *év* 'year' can be preceded both by *hány* 'how many' and *mennyi* 'how many, how much'. In the example, we can observe that Ica prefers *hány* 'how many' when she reflects upon the number of years she spent in the drama group.

In Example (22), Cili, who has recently got married, explains to the other participants how she and her husband can manage to visit all their relatives on Christmas Eve. In line 04, she interrupts the ongoing TCU within a segment which is not a recognisable word.

(22) (bea003n001: 152)

<pre>
01 C: és   akkor   újra: a   másik   családnál-   (.)   ugyanez a
       and   then   again   the   other   family.ADE   same   the
       'and then with the other family- (.) the same

02   felvonás hogy   vacsora   .hh   s   akko   má
       act   that   dinner   and   then   already
       act again there's a dinner .hh and then in this way we already

03   így   elég   rosszul   voltunk,   .h   és   akkor   már
       in.this.way   quite   badly   was.1PL.INDEF   and   then   already
       felt quite bad, .h and then

04   utána   így   együtt   vo-   vándoroltu:nk.
       afterwards   in.this.way   together   wandered.1PL.INDEF
       afterwards in this way **we were wandering** together.'
</pre>

C: and then with the other family- (.) the same act again there's a dinner .hh and then in
     this way we already felt quite bad, .h and then afterwards in this way **(replaced item)**
     we were wandering together.

In line 04, Cili replaces *vo-* with *vándoroltu:nk* 'we were wandering'. This time
we cannot identify any problems fixed by the replacing. On the basis of the investigated material, we can only say that when Cili constructs her turn so that it
performs the job it is designed to perform (cf. Drew, Walker, and Ogden 2013:
92), she replaces an item with another one.

As was mentioned earlier, repair can be initiated without an apparent error,
and nothing is excludable from the class *repairable* (Schegloff et al. 1977: 363).
Schegloff (2013: 47) notes that repairing is often merely altering: there are cases
when instead of fixing a problem, the speaker merely changes the turn-so-far
(see the differentiation between the terms *repair* and *correction* in Section 3.2).
According to *The Handbook of Conversation Analysis*, repair can be used as a resource for the interactional fine-tuning of the turn in the service of the particular
action the speaker designs it to perform (Kitzinger 2013: 242), i.e., specifically to
do interactional work without any problems to be fixed. I understand the term
interactional function as this 'interactional task-at-hand' that repair operations
can fulfil (Wilkinson and Weatherall 2011: 72).

Kitzinger (2013: 243) points out that downgrading the force of the action that
the turn implements is a frequently used way of interactionally fine-tuning a turn.
In Kitzinger's example, the speaker, who is a helpline caller responding to a question about her pain, downgrades her admission by replacing *is my f:-* with the
weaker formulation *mi(h)ght be my fault* (Example (23)).

(23) (Kitzinger 2013: 243)

```
1   Clt:   You're two years on and you've still go:t=
2   Mel:     [yeah]
3   Clt:   =[still  ]got pai:n.
4   Mel:   I mean part of it I have to sa:y is my f:-
5          mi(h)ght be my fault because I've been given
6          .hh exercises to [and I ]ha:rdly ever do=
7   Clt:                    [yeah ]
8   Mel:   = them…
```

The reverse interactional effect on the action is accomplished by using replacing
repairs in which the speaker substitutes a weaker element with a stronger one. In
Kitzinger's example, an advisor on a helpline tells the recipient that s/he is entitled
to change a healthcare provider. She replaces the permissive *can* with the stronger
have the absolute right to (Example (24)).

(24) (Kitzinger 2013: 243)

1	Clt:	If there's anybody that you fee:l .hhh
2		<u>is</u>n't supporting you then: **you can ch-**
3		**you have- you have the <u>ab</u>solute right to**
4		**ch<u>a</u>nge** that person

Jefferson (1974) suggests that substituting one word for another, if the substituted segment is not recognisably complete[4] but still recognisable, allows the speaker to produce an inappropriate[5] item without being interactionally accountable for it. She says that in these cases the speaker does not produce the word in question officially. In her example, the speaker replaces *k-* 'coloured' with *Negro woman*, and according to Jefferson, this can propose that 'I am not a liberal but am talking by reference to the fact that you are' (Jefferson 1974: 193) (Example (25)).

(25) (TRIO: 10)[6] (Jefferson 1974: 193)

Jean: Well, she said thet there was some woman thet-the-thet they were
        whh- had held up in the front there, thet they were poin'ing the gun at,
        'n everything, (0.4) a **k- Negro** woman.

Drew et al. (2013) establish three principles guiding turn design. Speakers design their talk to make it appropriate for its sequential environment, for the action they intend it to do, and for the recipient to whom it is addressed. In Example (26) below, the operation replacing is used to downgrade a formulation to make it appropriate for its sequential environment. Gábor, Pali, and Viola are discussing what they would do in an imagined situation where they have to decide whether to help a friend or not. The situation is as follows: you have a friend who has failed an exam eight times. If s/he fails once more, s/he will be dismissed from the university. Before the last exam, s/he asks you to go into one of the toilets of the university building with the exam topics worked out.[7] During the exam, after your friend has been given the topic titles, s/he plans to ask to go to the toilet and sneak the papers s/he needs back into the exam room. If the cheating comes to light, both of you will be dismissed from the university.

(26) (SZTEPSZI2: 953)

01 G:	*mit*	*mondtál*	*hogy*	*mért*	*mennél*	*be.*
	what.ACC	said.2SG.INDEF	that	why	go.COND.2SG.INDEF	PVB
	'why have you said you would go in.					

      (0.3)

02 G:	*már-*	*már-*	[*mármos*	*hogy-*	]
			now	that-	
	I	I	[I mean	that-	]

03 V: [*én   cs-*   ] *hát   ö: több: dolgot   is*
                         I   well   u:h   several   thing.ACC   also
                         [I   jus-   ] well, u:h I have said several things,

04   *mondtam,   egyrészt   annak   függvényében*
        said.1SG.INDEF   on.the.one.hand   that.GEN   dependent.POSS.3SG.INE
        on the one hand it depends on

05   *hogy   ő   hogy   győz   meg   engem*   (0.2)
        that   s/he   how   persuades   PVB   me
        how s/he persuades me (0.2)

06   *a   másik   az   meg   hogy   már   csak   a*   (.)
        the   other   that   and   that   even   just   the
        on the other hand (I would go in) even just (.)

07   *poén   kedvéér.   én: nem   szoktam   ilyeneket*
        joke   for.the.sake   I   not   used.1SG.INDEF   such.things.ACC
        for fun. I: usually don't do such things

08   *csinálni   és   ((laughing))   [most   ez*
        do.INF   and   now   this
        and   ((laughing))   [now   this

09 G: [*de   hogy te   nem   félted   a:*
                                             but   that you   not   fear.2SG.DEF   the
                                             [but don't you fear for your:

10   *merhogy   ne-   nem   félted   a   saját   helyzetedet?*
        because   no-   not   fear.2SG.DEF   the own   situation.POSS.2SG.ACC
        because don- don't you fear for your own position (at the university)?

        (1.5)

11 G: *merhogy   ez   egy   poén.   igen.*
        because   this   a   joke   yes
        because this is a joke. yes.

12 V: *nem.*
        no
        no.

13 G: *de   hogy   egy   egy   poén   kedvéért   fölál- ö*
        but   that   a   a   joke   for.the.sake   sacri- uh
        but for a a joke do you **sacri- uh**

14   **kockára   teszed**   *egyébként   a:?*
        cube.SUB   put.2SG.DEF   by.the.way   the
        risk, by the way, your (position at the university)?'

G: why have you said you would go in.
    (0.3)
G: I   I   [I mean that-]
V: [I jus-   ] well, u:h I have said several things, on the
    one hand it depends on how s/he persuades me (0.2) on the other
    hand (I would go in) even just (.) for fun. I: usually don't do such
    things and ((laughing))   [now this
G: [but don't you fear for your: because
    don- don't you fear for your own position (at the university)?
    (1.5)
G: because this is a joke. yes.
V: no.
G: but for a a joke do you **sacri- uh risk**, by the way, your (position at the university)?

In line 01, Gábor asks Viola to sum up her arguments for helping the friend.
When Viola says that she would do that even just for fun (lines 06–07), Gábor
finds it strange that she does not fear the potential threat to her status at the
university. In line 13, he starts to ask whether it is worth sacrificing one's own
university status for a joke; however, in the middle of the word *föláldozod* ('you
sacrifice') he breaks off (*fölál-* ('you sacri-')) and replaces it with the much weaker
kockára teszed ('you risk'). The reason for the substitution becomes understand-
able if we take into consideration the sequential environment of the repair. The
rejected selection *föláldozod* ('you sacrifice') means that Viola will in any case
be dismissed if she helps her friend. However, in the imagined situation it is not
certain that they will be caught; therefore, the turn is better constructed with
kockára teszed ('you risk').

The downgrading function of replacing can also be seen in Example (27), when
Linda shares her opinion about the frequency of theft. She says that it is enough
to leave a bag unattended in a bicycle basket, for it to get stolen.

(27) (SZTEPSZI8: 1089)

01 L: *alapból   az   hogy   valami   érték*
        basis.ELA   that   that   something   value
        'it is enough that something valuable

02   *ami: ott   van   szabadon   az   [így]*
        which   there   is   unattended   that   in.this.way
        which is left there unattended that [in this way]

03 B: [*azt*]
                                                        that.ACC
                                                        [it   ]

04   *így*   (.)   *biz* [*tos   hogy   nem   hagyod   ott.*]
       in.this.way   sure   that   not   leave.2SG.DEF   there
       is su[re that you won't leave it there.]

05 L: [*tök   mindegy   ká*]*bé   hogy*
                                           very   no.matter   roughly   that
                                           [we can say that it doesn't matter at   ] all

06   *mi   te*[*hát*]   (.) **most   általá- vagy én legalábbis mindig ezt**   =
       what   that.is   now   usua-   or   I   at.least   always   this.ACC
       what it is, that [is] (.) **usua- or at least I always**=

07 B: [*ja.*]
                                yeah
                                [yeah.]

08 L: = **tapasztalom**   *hogy   ha   most   a   biciklikosárba*
            experience.1SG.DEF   that   if   now   the   bicycle.basket.INE
         = **see that** if there is a bag in a bicycle basket

09   *van   egy   zacskó   nem   tudja   mi   van*
       is   a   bag   not   knows.DEF   what   is
       s/he doesn't know what is

10   *benne   akkor   is   elviszi.*
       in.it   then   also   PVB.takes.DEF
       in it but s/he will still take it.'

L: it is enough that something valuable which is left there unattended that [in this way]
B: [it   ]
     is su[re that you won't leave it there.   ]
L: [we can say that it doesn't matter at] all what it is, that [is   ] (.) **usua- or =**
B: [yeah.]
L: **=at least I always see that** if there is a bag in a bicycle basket s/he doesn't know
     what is in it but s/he will still take it.

In line 06, when Linda refers to the frequency of theft, she at first seems to be saying that this is the usual way things happen. Nonetheless, before the last syllable
of *általában* ('usually'), she initiates repair with a cut-off and replaces the word
with the weaker *vagy én legalábbis mindig ezt tapasztalom* ('or at least I always see
that'), which restricts her opinion to her own experience. This repair does not fix a
problem in speaking, hearing, or understanding the talk, but rather alters the turn
in an interactionally consequential way: by employing the replacing operation,
Linda reduces her responsibility for the radical criticism. The importance of the
interactional work these kinds of repair perform is indicated by Linda's attempt to

decrease the power of her critical remark[8] in spite of the fact that Boglárka, one of her co-participants, strongly agrees with her (lines 03–04, and 07).

As was noted earlier, the speaker has to design the turn taking into consideration not only its position in the sequence (see Example (26)) and the action it is intended to achieve (see Example (27)), but also the particular recipient it is addressed to (Drew et al. 2013). In Example (28), we can see how the speaker employs replacing repair so as to make the turn appropriate for the recipient. In Hungarian, address is possible in several forms (Domonkosi 2002). There are two polite equivalents of 'you': *maga* (plural: *maguk*) and *ön* (plural: *önök*). *Ön* is used exclusively in formal situations, when the speaker addresses somebody who s/he is not on familiar terms with, while *maga* is less formal than *ön* but more formal than *te* and can be used both in formal and informal situations. Both *maga* and *ön* occur with a third person verb. In Example (28), two young women, Enikő and Márta are talking to an older man, Tibor. Enikő asks Tibor how he has spent Christmas and how it is usually celebrated at his place.

(28) (bea004f003: 200)

```
01  E:  arra        gondoltunk          Mártá(.)val      hogy   ö:
        that.SUB    thought.1PL.INDEF   Márta.COM        that   u:h
        'Márta and I have been thinking about u:h

02      szeretnénk          önt         megkérdezni    hogy  a     karácsonyt
        like.COND.1PL.DEF   you.ACC     PVB.ask.INF    that  the   Christmas.ACC
        asking you how (.)

03      azt         (.)  hogyan   töltötte         ön?    meg   hogyan
        that.ACC         how      spent.3SG.DEF    you    and   how
        you spent Christmas? and how

04      szokott   ma-    önöknél      zajlani?       (.)  az    egész
        used      yo-    you.PL.ADE   happen.INF          the   whole
        is it usually celebrated at yo- your place? (.) the whole

05      (.)  ünnep?
             holiday
        (.)  Christmas holiday?

        (1.0)

06  T:  na      jó.
        now     good
        alright.

        (2.0)
```

07 T: *akkor   kezdjék   maguk!*
        then   begin.IMP.3PL.DEF   you.PL
        but you should begin!'

E: Márta and I have been thinking about u:h asking you how (.) you spent
    Christmas? and how is it usually celebrated at **yo- your** place? (.) the whole
    (.) Christmas holiday?
    (1.0)
T: alright.
    (2.0)
T: but you should begin!

Enikő addresses Tibor three times in the example (in lines 02, 03, and 04). While
on the first two occasions she uses *ön*, in line 04 she selects at first *maguknál*, but,
after the first syllable (*ma-*), she replaces it with *önöknél* 'at your place', which
increases the distance between Enikő and Tibor. This also indicates that the use
of *maga* and *ön* should not alternate in the same conversation when addressing
the same co-participant. In line 07, the old man also addresses the young women,
but, in contrast to Enikő, he uses the less formal *maguk*, which establishes a hierarchical relationship between the women and him.

5.2 Recycling

The second repair operation on which I aim to build my comparative investigation is *recycling*. According to Schegloff (2013: 59), the term *recycling* refers to a
speaker's repeating some stretch of talk that they have previously uttered, most
typically a stretch which has been said just before. This definition refers to all uses
of recycling, including those cases when it is not a repair operation, for example, when the repeated element(s) only frame the repair (e.g., when the speaker
repeats a word before replacing) (Example (29)), or when the second utterance
emphasises or stresses the first (Rieger 2003: 51) (Example (30)).

(29) (Schegloff 2013: 44)

Bee: was I sid <u>no</u> I sid but we're supposetuh know what it
       is **fuh Weh-** .hh yihknow **fuh tihday's** class. 'n,

(30) (bea002f002: 83)

01 B: *az   nem   volt   könnyű   megtanulni.*=
        that   not   was.3SG   easy   PVB.learn.INF
        'it wasn't easy to learn that. =

02   = *főleg*   *az*   *ilyen*   *(.)*   *beparkolásos*   *manőver*
         especially   the   such   parking   manoeuvre
         = especially this kind of (.) parking manoeuvre

03   *ilyen*   *(.)*   *mittöminek*   *hívják*   *ezt*   *.h*
         such   whatever.DAT   call.3PL.DEF   this.ACC
         this kind of (.) whatever they call it .h

04 A: [*mhm*]
         uhm
         [uhm]

05 C: [*de*]   *ez*   *a*   *szervofék*   *ez-*   *ez*
         but   this   the   servo.brake   this   this
         [but   ] this servo brake isn'- isn't it

06   *nem*   *veszélyes?*   *hogy így*   *csak* *>nyomod*   *nyomod<*
         not   dangerous   that   in.this.way   just   push.2SG.DEF   push.2SG.DEF
         dangerous? that in this way you just >**push it push it**<

07   *és*   *akkor*   *mikor*   *állsz*   *meg?*   *=*   *vagy*
         and   then   when   stop.2SG.INDEF   PVB   or
         and then when do you stop?=or'

B: it wasn't easy to learn that. = especially this kind of (.) parking
     manoeuvre this kind of (.) whatever they call it .h
A: [uhm   ]
C: [but   ] this servo brake isn'- isn't it dangerous? that in this way you just
     >**push it push it**< and then when do you stop?=or

In line 06, *nyomod nyomod* 'push it push it' is delivered by the speaker more rap-
idly than usual. This way of delivery expresses the continuity and intensity of
using a servo brake, rather than being a repair operation.

   Furthermore, if the second utterance of the same item diverges from the first
only in a prosodic respect, the consecutive usage of the same element(s) may be
a repair operation, but rather a replacing than a recycling (Schegloff 2013: 60). In
Example (31), Shelley recycles the entire run-up to the word 'he's', but in the last
production, a heavy stress is given to 'he:'s'.

(31) (Schegloff 2013: 61)

01 Shl: So: I mean it's <u>n</u>ot becuz **he's**– **he's**– I mean it's
02   <u>n</u>ot becuz **he:'s** not going, it's becuz (0.5) his
03   <u>m</u>oney's not: (0.5) <u>fun</u>ding me.
04 Deb: <u>o</u>kay,

Recycling as a repair operation can be used at the emergence of overlapping talk in order to deal with possible problems in hearing or understanding caused by simultaneous talk (Schegloff 2013: 59–60; cf. Schegloff 1987) or at the emergence of inattentiveness in order to attract the nongazing recipients' gaze (Goodwin 1980). While in the former case the speaker repeats some stretch of talk in order to say it in the clear (Schegloff 2013: 60), in the latter the function of the repair operation is to elicit gaze from recipients. To these functions of recycling as a repair operation Fox et al. (2009: 75) add another: it can also serve as a device for delaying the next item due, e.g., when the speaker needs time to select the appropriate next word or choose between alternatives (Jefferson 1974). Although the former functions also delay the talk that follows literally, in those cases the repair operation deals with a problem concerning the repeated talk: the potentially compromised hearing of the stretch of talk uttered in interactionally problematic moments (overlap or inattentiveness) (Schegloff 2009: 386). That is, at the emergence of overlapping talk and inattentiveness, delaying the next item due is only a by-product of the repair operation of recycling. The Hungarian corpus contains recycling repairs which combine the functions described by Schegloff (2013) and Fox et al. (2009). In Example (32), Ábel, Boglárka, and Linda are talking about Hungarian music bands which have become famous outside Hungary.

(32) (SZTEPSZI8: 1062)

```
01 Á: sok       olyan    zenekar van  amúgy    aki:    sokat
      many      such     band    is   anyway   who     a.lot.ACC
      'there are a lot of bands by the way who:

02    játszik   külföldön [tehát  tehát    tehát   olyan]ok  is=
      plays     abroad    that.is that.is  that.is such.PL   also
      play a lot abroad [that is that is that is even band]s=

03 L:                    [hát   ige:n.  tényleg  sokan. ]
                         well   yes     really   many
                         [well ye:s. there are really a lot.   ]

04 Á: =ak-    akik    a [kik   akik     akik ]=
      wh-     who.PL  who.PL  who.PL   who.PL
      =wh- who wh[o who who]=

05 B:                    [de          lehe-        ]
                         but          maybe-
                         [but         maybe-       ]
```

06 Á: =*Magyar*[*orszá*]*gon   annyira   nem   is   durván   ismertek.*
        Hungary.SUP   so.much   not   also   roughly   known.PL
        =are not so well-known in Hun[gar]y.'

07 B: [*ja:.*]
                    yeah
                    [ye:ah]

Á: there are a lot of bands by the way who: play a lot abroad
    [**that is that is that is** even band]s wh- who=
L: [well ye:s. there are really a lot.   ]
Á: =**wh**[**o who who**] in Hun[gar]y are not so well-known.
B: [but maybe-]   [ye:ah.]

In lines 02 and 04, Ábel recycles his talk which overlaps Linda and Boglárka's talk, respectively, but not in the way Schegloff (2013: 60) describes this kind of recycling. That is to say, it is not the repeated talk that Ábel produces in the clear. The stretch of talk which is produced in the clear is the talk that follows the recycling. Therefore, in these cases, the repair operation serves as a device for delaying the talk that follows in order to say it in the clear. In this way, the recycling deals with a problem concerned not with the repeated but with the upcoming talk: by recycling, the speaker can avoid[9] a possibly compromised hearing of the upcoming talk. This analysis is supported by the direction of Ábel's gaze, which he changes during his overlapping talk. Realising that Boglárka has started to talk simultaneously, he recycles *akik* 'who' twice, while directing his gaze towards her. Boglárka responds to this by a cut-off (*de lehe-* 'but maybe-') and lets him continue his talk.

Schegloff (2009: 385–386) argues against the proposal made by Fox et al. (2009). He rejects the idea that recycling, if its sole function is to delay the next item due, can be interpreted as a repair operation. He says that there are other practices which also delay the next item due, such as *uh(m)*, *y'know*, and silence,[10] which can occur separately or together 'in the environment of repair' (Schegloff 2009: 385). He asks: 'What then is done by recycling *distinctively*?' (Schegloff 2009: 386, emphasis original). That is to say, Schegloff argues here that the practices such as *uh(m)*, *y'know*, and silence can have the same function as recycling, but they can occur *in the environment of* repair, they themselves therefore are not repair operations. And indeed, they are listed in *The Handbook of Conversation Analysis* as practices of repair initiation (Kitzinger 2013: 239, see above in Section 3.2). In other words, Schegloff's problem is that, although the practices listed above do the same thing as recycling, they are not repair operations; consequently, recycling with the sole function of delaying the next item due cannot be interpreted as a repair operation either. Now, we are confronted with p-inconsistency in the conversation analytic literature, which means that both a statement and its negation are made plausible by some (different) source (Kertész and Rákosi 2012: 130–134; 2014: 29–32; Section 4.3.1). According to Schegloff (2009), recycling with the same delaying function as the practices such as *uh(m)*, *y'know*, and silence should not be interpreted as a repair operation, because the practices listed above are not repair operations either. However, according to Fox et al. (2009), recycling with the sole function of delaying the next item due should be interpreted as a repair operation. As a problem-solving strategy, I will apply the Combinative Strategy (Kertész and Rákosi 2012: 153–161; 2014: 35–37; Section 4.3.2). I keep both Schegloff's (2009: 385–386) and Fox et al.'s (2009: 75) statements as co-existing alternatives, but I separate two domains of occurrences of the practices such as *uh(m)*, *y'know*, and silence listed by Schegloff (2009: 385–386) and Kitzinger (2013: 239). I propose that if their function is to indicate a 'possible disjunction with the immediately preceding talk' (Schegloff 2000: 207), then they should be interpreted as repair initiation practices (see Example (26), line 13). However, as Schegloff (2009: 385) suggests, there are cases when their function is the same as the function of recycling when it delays the next item due. My proposal here is that instead of *not* regarding these occurrences of recycling as repair operations, the practices such as *uh(m)*, *y'know*, and silence should be regarded as repair operations when they are used as devices for delaying the talk that follows. The basis of this argumentation is the concept of repair: it involves the practices whereby a co-interactant interrupts her/his ongoing turn-at-talk to attend to possible trouble in speaking, hearing, or understanding the talk. That is, if recycling or the practices such as *uh(m)*, *y'know*, and silence are employed solely to delay the next item due, and by this action the speaker attends to possible trouble in speaking, hearing, or understanding the talk, then we should interpret them as repair and repair operations.[11]

Lerner (2013: 105) suggests that the turn-constructional delaying strategies used when searching for a word can display hesitation or unease about what the speaker is about to say. Hesitation may appear before a predictably delicate term or before a term that is part of a turn-constructional unit formulating a delicate matter or implementing a delicate action, when the speaker, for example, negatively evaluates someone's character or actions (Lerner 2013: 104). This way of delivery can show that, although the speaker is loath to say something, s/he still voices it (cf. Whitehead 2009). In Example (33), the delicate action the speaker engages in is the delivery of self-praise. Szili (2004: 283) finds that Hungarian speakers follow the principle of modesty (Leech 1983) when replying to compliments on their personal performances (see also Szili 2010). Moreover, according to Szili (2000: 276), self-praise is generally not preferred in Hungarian culture. Therefore, the delivery of self-praise relating to the speaker's personal performance may make her/him feel uneasy in Hungarian conversations. In the example, three teacher trainees, Bogi, Feri, and Eszter are talking about their teaching practices. Feri tells the others that after his teaching exam, which is always the last lesson of the teaching practice, one of his students went up to him and gave a positive opinion on his work. Since Feri has not been asked earlier in the conversation whether his teaching practice was successful or not, it is of his own accord that he shares his student's opinion with the others. This means that his telling is a delivery of self-praise in the context of Hungarian culture.

(33) (bea007f005: 430)

```
01  F:  és     aztán: (.)   tehát    ö     már      a     már     a:
        and    then         that.is  uh    already  the   already the
        'and then: (.) that is uh after after my

02      a     vizsgatanításom              után    tehát     amikor     már
        the   exam.teaching.POSS.1SG       after   that.is   when       already
        my teaching exam that is when he

03      tényleg   semmi      tétje             nem    volt        annak
        really    nothing    risk.POSS.3SG     not    was.3SG     that.GEN
        really didn't take any risk

04      hogy    milyen      véleményt        mond     a      .hh    arról      (.)
        that    what.kind   opinion.ACC      tells    the           that.DEL
        telling his opinion on the .hh on (.)

05      amilyen    én     voltam        velü:k,        .hh    ((swallow))
        kind       I      was.1SG.INDEF with.them
        what I was like with them, .hh ((swallow))

06      akkor     azt        mondta         hogy   hogy   hogy   (.)  hogy
        then      that.ACC   told.3SG.DEF   that   that   that        that
        then he told that that that (.) that

07      tetszettek          (.)   ne>kik  =  jó<    hát    a:z egész  osztály
        were.pleasing.3PL          to.them    OK     well   the whole  class
        they liked (.) them (the lessons)=well it's OK he spoke

08      nevében             beszélt   dehát   ige:n   legyünk
        name.POSS.3SG.INE   spoke     but     yes     be.IMP.1PL.INDEF
        on behalf of the whole class but we should be

09      realisták    tehát     ö     NEki      nagyon
        realist.PL   that.is   uh    for.him   very.much
        realists that is uh HE
```

10	*tetszett*	*a-* **ahogy**	*tanítottam*
	was.pleasing.3SG	the.way	taught.1SG.INDEF

liked **th- the** way I taught very much'

F: and then: (.) that is uh after after my my teaching exam that is when he really didn't take any risk telling his opinion on the .hh on (.) what I was like with them, **.hh ((swallow))** **then he told that that that (.) that they liked (.) them (the lessons)**=well it's OK he spoke on behalf of the whole class but we should be realists that is uh <u>HE</u> liked **th- the** way I taught very much

In lines 01–04, Feri emphasises that the student must have been honest, since after the last lesson Feri would not be able to give him better marks for the positive remark. The first occasion on which Feri refers to himself and his teaching performance is in line 04, where he shares with his co-participants what the student's opinion was about. At first, it seems that he is about to use the noun phrase *véleményt mond a* ('his opinion on the'), but, after an audible inhalation, he replaces the initiated NP with the clause *arról (.) amilyen én voltam velü:k* ('on (.) what I was like with them'). This means that instead of referring to his performance directly, he selects a circumlocution. The analysis of this replacing as a first sign of Feri's possible unease is supported by the way in which the TCU is completed. Before Feri refers to his success, there is an audible inhalation and a swallow in line 05. Then in line 06, just prior to the self-praising expression (*tetszettek nekik* 'they liked them'), he recycles *hogy* 'that' three times, with a pause before the last recycling. The self-praising expression also contains a pause. The assumption that these phenomena result from Feri's unease about delivering self-praise is strengthened by the extension of the turn: after he talks about the positive comment he had received, he quickly adds that this was probably just the student's own opinion, even though the student allegedly spoke on behalf of the whole class. This modest comment, which may serve as a compensation for the earlier immodesty, is delivered as a coherent prosodic unit with the earlier part of speech (see the symbol = at the transition-relevance place in line 07). Feri also speeds up just prior to the potential end of the TCU, i.e., he rushes through the transition-relevance place (see the symbol > < in line 07).[12] This strategy may refer to his motivation to secure another unit of talk for delivering a modest comment without recipient intervention. His last self-reflection in line 10 also contains a recycling (*a- ahogy tanítottam* 'the- the way I taught'). All these turn-constructional delaying practices alter the turn in some interactionally consequential way, and their analysis makes it probable that their function is to display Feri's unease about what he is about to say during the delivery of self-praise. This seems to be a culture-specific interactional function in Hungarian.

Hesitating before a critical judgment may also express the speaker's unease about what s/he is about to say (Lerner 2013: 104) and therefore decrease the power of the critical assessment. In Examples (34) and (35), Móni, Attila, and Lilla are talking about their attitudes toward alcohol and drugs. In Example (34), Móni tells the others why she has not tried any kind of drugs: she saw their effects on her friends. In line 09, she closes her opinion with a strong critical judgment and uses the expression *undorító* 'disgusting'.

(34) (SZTEPSZI3: 856)

01 M: *és   például   a   drogokat.   egyszerűen   nem   próbáltam*
        and   for.example   the   drug.PL.ACC   simply   not   tried.1SG.DEF
        'and I have simply never tried for example drugs.

02   *ki   soha   azért   mert   láttam   a*
        PVB   never   that.CAU   because   saw.1SG.DEF   the
        because I saw

03   *barátaimat   hogy   hogy   ö: egy   normális   ember*
        friends.POSS.1SG.ACC   that   that   u:h   a   normal   man
        my friends that that u:h a normal human being

04   *egyszerűen   (.)   úgy   el   tud   távolodni*
        simply   so.much   PVB   can   move.away.INF
        can simply become so estranged

05   *és   annyira: embertelen   lesz   attól   amikor*
        and   so.much   inhuman   becomes   that.ABL   when
        and so: inhuman because of

06   *drogozik,   hogy   ez   engem   totál   visszataszított*
        uses.drugs   that   this   me   totally   repelled
        using drugs, that totally repelled me

07   *és   nem   is   ilyen   szülői   tiltásra   hanem*
        and   not   also   such   parent.ADJDER   forbidding.SUB   but
        and not because my parents forbade me to do that but

08   *ez   (.)   ez   ez   számomra   úgymond*
        this   this   this   for.me   so.to.say
        because **this (.) this this** was so to say

09   *undorító   volt*
        disgusting   was.3SG
        disgusting for me'

M: and I have simply never tried for example drugs. because I saw my friends that that u:h a normal human being can simply become so estranged and so: inhuman because of using drugs, that totally repelled me and not because my parents forbade me to do that but because **this (.) this this** was so to say disgusting for me

Before using the delicate expression *undorító* 'disgusting' in line 09, Móni employs the double recycling of the subject (*ez ez ez* 'this this this') with a pause. Since using the word *undorító* 'disgusting' is a very strong negative evaluation of someone's behaviour, Móni may be loath to voice it, which supports the idea that the double recycling and the pause preceding it are delaying strategies. This is further supported by the observation that, beyond these turn-constructional delaying practices, Móni uses other mitigating devices as well (*számomra* 'for me', *úgymond* 'so to say') in the delivery of her critical judgment. These practices, however, do not interrupt the ongoing turn-at-talk, and thus cannot be analysed as repair.

Examples (35) and (36) show that recycling in itself can also fulfil the interactional function Lerner (2013) describes, and thus alter the turn in an interactionally consequential way. In Example (35), Móni, Attila, and Lilla are discussing their attitudes toward alcohol.

(35) (SZTEPSZI3: 816)

```
01  L:  én      mindenféle    alkoholt       elítélek.
        I       all.kinds     alcohol.ACC    condemn.1SG.INDEF
        'I condemn all kinds of alcohol.

02          te[hát     személyes    tapasztalat    tehát.
        that.is        personal     experience     that.is
        that [is, it is a personal experience, so.

03  A:      [tehát    te      te      egyáltalán    nem (      )?
        that.is       you     you     at.all        not
        [so you you don't (      ) at all?

04  M:      [jó      de      te      antialkoholis [ta     vagy    úgyhogy.
        good         but     you     nondrinker          are      so
        [OK, but you   are a          non-drin[ker, so.

05  L:                                         [Igen.
                                            Yes
                                            [Yes.

06  A:  ja      hogy     te     egyál [talán    [nem     (        ).
        oh      that     you    at.all          not
        oh, so you don't (        )    [at      [all.

07  L:                                  [    tel [jesen.    tehát    hogy   (.)  nem.
                                        totally            that.is   that         not
                                        [    to  [tally. that is, I (.) don't.
```

08 M: [*totál   nem   iszik*
                                                    totally   not   drinks
                                                    [she totally doesn't drink

09   *alkoholt   semmit.*
        alcohol.ACC   nothing.ACC
        alcohol at all.

10 A: ↑*ja::*   *ér* [*tem.*
        oh   understand.1SG.DEF
        ↑o::h I under [stand.

11 L: [*én   én   nem   tudom   ezt   tolerálni,*
                            I   I   not   can.1SG.DEF   this.ACC   tolerate.INF
                            [I I cannot tolerate this,

12   *de   ez   az   én   magánügyem.*
        but   this   the   I   private.matter.POSS.1SG
        but this is my private matter.

13 A: *ja   jó   oké   én   ezt   elfogadom.*   (.)
        well   good   OK   I   this.ACC   accept.1SG.DEF
        well, it's good, OK, I accept this. (.)

14   [*ezen*
        this.SUP
        [on this

15 M: [*egyébként   (0.3)   én   azt   még   úgy   úgy*   (.)
        by.the.way   I   that.ACC   still   in.a.way   in.a.way
        [by the way (0.3) I can still (tolerate) it in a way in a way

16   *tudom   (.)   hogyha:,   mittudomén,   tényleg   elmegy*
        can.1SG.DEF   if   whatever   in.fact   PVB.goes
        if, in fact, s/he goes to a party or whatever

17   *buliba   és   akko   (.)   berúgott.   kész.   de   amikor*
        party.ILL   and   then   got.drunk   ready   but   when
        and then (.) s/he's got drunk. it's done. but when

18   *amikor   ez   a   totál   nem   tud   magáról.*
        when   this   the   totally   not   knows   her/himself.DEL
        when s/he doesn't know anything about himself/herself.

19   *semmi   képe   nincs   az   e*[*gész világról,*   .h
        nothing   idea.POSS.3SG   is.not   the   whole   world.DEL
        s/he doesn't have any idea [of reality, .h

20 L: [*és   ráadásul   ha*
                                                                          and   additionally if
                                                                          [and additionally, if

21   *lány   szerintem   az   még   inkább   meg* [*alázó.*
        girl   I.think   that   even   rather   degrading
        she is a girl, in my opinion it is even more de[grading.

22 M: [*és*
                                                                    and
                                                                    [and

23   *hány   és   neked   kell   rajta   segíteni,*
        throws.up   and   you   must   her   help.INF
        s/he throws up and you must help her/him,

24   *na   az   az   az   má   szerintem*
        well   that   that   that   already   I.think
        well **that that that** I think already

25   *megint   a   gáz   kategória.*
        again   the   gas[13]   category
        is the gas category.'

L: I condemn all kinds of alcohol. that [is, it is a personal experience, so.
A: [so you you don't (   ) at all?
M: [OK, but you are a non-drin [ker, so.
L: [Yes.
A: oh, so you don't ( ) [at [all.
L: [to [tally. that is, I (.) don't.
M: [she totally doesn't drink alcohol at all.
A: ↑o::h I under [stand.
L: [I I cannot tolerate this, but this is my private matter.
A: well, it's good, OK, I accept this. (.)   [on this
M: [by the way (0.3) I can still (tolerate)
    it in a way in a way if, in fact, s/he goes to a party or whatever and then (.)
    s/he's got drunk. it's done. but when when s/he doesn't know anything
    about himself/herself. s/he doesn't have any idea [of reality, .h
L: [and additionally, if she is a
    girl, in my opinion it is even more de [grading.
M: [and s/he throws up and you
    must help her/him, well **that that that** I think already is the gas category.

While Lilla condemns all kinds of alcoholic beverages, Móni accepts alcohol consumption to a certain extent. In lines 15–25, she explains what kind of behaviour she can and cannot tolerate when somebody is drunk in her company. In lines 24–25, she closes her opinion with a strong critical judgment on the behaviour she cannot stand. The delivery of this judgment takes place with the double recycling of the subject (*az az az* 'that that that') and the use of other mitigating devices: *na* ('well'), *má* ('already') and *szerintem* ('I think'). The delaying function of the recycling is supported by the direction of Móni's gaze. She does not look at any of the other participants until the last uttering of the recycled item, when she directs her gaze towards Attila (who is selected as the next speaker) and finishes her turn with a final intonational contour (indicated by a dot in the transcription).

The Hungarian corpus shows that displaying hesitancy or unease about what the speaker is about to say (Lerner 2013) may not only occur during the delivery of self-praise and criticism, but also in avoiding offensive language. In Example (36), Ági, Zsuzsi, and Marcsi are talking about a freestyle rapper who has mobility difficulties.

(36) (SZTEPSZI2: 725)

01 Á: *csak　　az　　a　　bajom*　　　　　(.)　*ezzel　　a*
　　　only　　that　the　trouble.POSS.1SG　　　this.INS　the
　　　'my only problem with this

02 　　*gyerekkel,　hogy　ilyen: totál　elszállt.　　　tehát　　legalábbis　így*
　　　guy.INS　　　that　such　totally　overweening　that.is　at.least　　this.way
　　　guy is that he is a smart alec. so at least

03 　　*ránézésre,　és　　emiatt　　　　unszimpatikus,　emiatt*
　　　outwardly　　and　for.this.reason　unlikable　　　for.this.reason
　　　he seems to be, and for this reason he doesn't appeal to me, for this reason

04 　　*már　　　a　　tehetségét　　　　sem　　　tudom*
　　　already　the　talent.POSS.3SG.ACC　also.not　can.1SG.DEF
　　　I cannot appreciate his talent any more,

05 　　*értékelni,　mondjuk　nem　mintha　a　　freestyleosokat*
　　　appreciate.INF　by.the.way　not　as.if　the　freestyle.ADJDER.PL.ACC
　　　by the way we cannot say that I appreciate freestyle rappers

06 　　*értékelném　　　　　mert　szerintem　nem　tehetségek,*
　　　appreciate.COND.1SG.DEF　because　I.think　　not　talents
　　　because I don't think they are talented,

07 M: *én　ennek　　tök　　　örülök　　　　mert*
　　　I　this.DAT　very.much　feel.joy.1SG.INDEF　because
　　　I am so happy about that (the rapper's success) because

08	*szerintem*	*ilyen*	*óriási*	*(.)*	*hátrányokkal*	*indul.*
	I.think	such	huge		disadvantages.INS	starts

I think he starts out with huge disadvantages.

09	*tehát*	*baromi*	*hendikeppel*	***hogy***	***hogy***	***hogy***	*olyan*
	that.is	enormous	handicap.INS	that	that	that	such

that is with an enormous handicap **that that that** he is

10	*amilyen*
	such

like that'

Á: my only problem with this guy is that he is a smart alec. so at least he seems to be, and for this reason he doesn't appeal to me, for this reason I cannot appreciate his talent any more, by the way we cannot say that I appreciate freestyle rappers because I don't think they are talented,

M: I am so happy about that (the rapper's success) because I think he starts out with huge disadvantages. that is with an enormous handicap **that that that** he is like that

In line 09, before Marcsi refers to the rapper's disability, she recycles *hogy* 'that' twice. This may indicate her unease about referring to the disorder in an inoffensive way. At last, she decides to refer to the disability without naming it.

Examples (33), (34), (35), and (36) show that when recycling and the practices such as *uh(m)*, *y'know*, and silence are used for delaying the talk that follows, they can be a part of a search, which is regarded as a repair operation in its own right by Schegloff (2013). However, even in these cases these practices do not occur 'in the environment of repair' (Schegloff 2009: 385), but they are the repair itself. This makes the proposal of Fox et al. (2009: 75) plausible: if the speaker employs recycling as a device for delaying the next item due, and s/he does this in order to attend to possible trouble in speaking, hearing, or understanding the talk, then we should interpret recycling as a repair operation.[14]

The third repair operation on which I will build my model describing repair operations relative to each other is inserting.

5.3 Inserting

Inserting is a practice in which a speaker halts the talk-in-progress in order to go back and add something else to the turn before resuming (Wilkinson and Weatherall 2011: 65). In this repair operation, the new element(s) that the speaker inserts into the turn-so-far are recognisable as other than what the speaker was to say as the next element(s) (Schegloff 2013: 45). In Example (37), Márton shares his adventures in finding the location of his driving test. In line 06, he inserts a location adverb into the TCU.

(37) (bea001f001: 16)

01 M: *visszamentem.   mondták   hogy   az*
         back.went.1SG.INDEF   told.3PL.DEF   that   the
         'I went back. they told me that

02   *elején   van   valami: .h   autós-   >me*
         front.POSS.3SG.SUP   is   something   car.ADJDER   because
         at the beginning of it there is some kind of .h driving- >because

03   *mondtam   hogy   nekem   vizsgázni   kéne<   van   ott*
         told.1SG.DEF   that   for.me   take.an.exam.INF   should is   there
         I told them that I should take an exam< at that place there is

04   *valami: autós   intézet.   =   valami*
         something   car.ADJDER   institute   something
         some kind of driving institute. = some kind of

05   *autóbiztonsági   mittomén   milyen   intézet   volt*
         car.security.ADJDER   whatever   what.kind   institute   was.3SG
         car security I don't know what kind of institute was

06   *ott.   .hh   **mondt-   ott**   **mondták**   hogy   á:*
         there   to-   there   told.3PL.DEF   that   oh[15]
         there. .hh **they to- there they told** me that <u>o:h</u>

07   *nem   nem.   =   aszondja   menjen   vissza*
         not   not   says   go.IMP.3SG.INDEF   back
         no no. = s/he says you should go back'

M: I went back. they told me that at the beginning of it there is some kind of .h
     driving- >because I told them that I should take an exam< at that place there
     is some kind of driving institute. = some kind of car security I don't know
     what kind of institute was there. .hh **they to- there they told** me that <u>o:h</u> no
     no. = s/he says you should go back

After Márton articulates *mondt-* 'they to-' in line 06, he initiates repair by a cut-off and incorporates an additional word (the location adverb *ott* 'there'). Since the turn would not be appropriately articulated without repeating the element which has already been articulated before the inserting, the inserted word is always framed by repeating some of the talk around it (cf. Kitzinger 2013: 239). As this repetition constitutes a part of the repair segment, i.e., the operation would not work without it, we can say that inserting inherently includes the repetition of one or more element(s). In this example above, it is not the case that something is wrong and has to be fixed in the talk. Márton initiates the inserting of the location adverb *ott* 'there' in order to specify the place where he was helped with advice about where to go to take his driving test. Inserting is a repair operation which often merely alters the turn instead of fixing an apparent problem in it. When this is the case, the turn is not to be ungrammatical, i.e., the added word is not missing, but the speaker finds that what s/he has just said could be better realised by that alteration (Schegloff 2013: 47).

Analysing more than 500 inserting repairs in British, New Zealand, and U.S. English, Wilkinson and Weatherall (2011) differentiate between the *repairing* action that inserting can accomplish (e.g., specifying, intensifying, and other modifications) and the several *interactional* actions being served by the modifications, such as highlighting newsworthiness, strengthening an account, accounting for an assessment, providing evidence for an assertion, etc. Wilkinson and Weatherall (2011: 88) suggest, however, that while there are typical repairing actions (e.g., specifying or intensifying) inserting may accomplish, the interactional actions listed above are not specific to inserting, but tend to be case-specific, and should be analysed on a case-by-case basis.

Intensifying by using inserting can have the same upgrading effect on the action as replacing repairs do when they are used for intensifying (Kitzinger 2013: 243). In Wilkinson and Weatherall's example (Example (38)), the presenter of a radio arts programme inserts *spanking* before *new* when naming a museum (*spanking new (.) Wedgwood museum*). This intensifies the newness of the museum, and thereby highlights the newsworthiness of the report (2011: 81). The authors point out that intensifying through the inserting of words like *completely, really,* or *extremely* can result in an *extreme case formulation* (2011: 81; see, also, Pomerantz 1986).

(38) (Wilkinson and Weatherall 2011: 81)

Pre: I'm n͟o͟w at thee **ne͟:w (0.2) spa͟n͟king ne͟w** (.) We͟dgwood
       museum in Stoke on Tre:nt. hh A:: (.) ve͟ry swi͟sh
       ne:w modern buil:ding

When there are two or more possible referents available, inserting a specifying term can fix a possible problem in understanding (e.g., inserting *Cary* before *cemetery* (Wilkinson and Weatherall 2011: 73) (Example (39)).

(39) (Wilkinson and Weatherall 2011: 73)

Phi: at uhm (0.2) Yeh the service's at uhm twelve o'clock 'n
       then: the .hwhhhh the: uh:m (0.5) it'll be in **the ce͟h-**
       the Cary cemet'ry afterwards

Specifying through inserting may also be in the service of an interactional task-at-hand, when, instead of differentiating between two or more possible referents, it alerts the recipient to the relevance of the referent being of a specific type. For instance, inserting *micro* before *habitats* in the description of a zoo can provide evidence for the assertion that the zoo offers vast amounts of space for the animals (Wilkinson and Weatherall 2011: 79) (Example (40)).

(40) (Wilkinson and Weatherall 2011: 79)

Dav: The impo̲rtance of this enclo:sure is that .hh uh:m
        we gave him opportu̲nity .hh to really display his
        who̲:le (.) behavioural repertoire. .hh The
        comple̲xi:ty of the enclo:sure .hhh the who̲le
        different **ha̲bitats mi̲crohabitats** in the enclo:sure.

(41) (Wilkinson and Weatherall 2011: 78)

DR: They steal your bloody **sh: Doc Mar:tens sh**oe:s
       an : ::: wh:: whatever you've got o:n it's-

In Example (41), the modification of the reference formulation serves to account for the speaker's earlier assessment in the conversation, according to which Cuba Mall is a dangerous street. Here, the modification proposes that the thieves 'working' in the street steal branded goods instead of basic things (Wilkinson and Weatherall 2011: 78).

Luke and Wei Zhang (2010: 175) provide examples of inserting in Mandarin Chinese. Inserting *ying* 'by force, against one's will' before *la shangqu le* 'dragged me up', the speaker accounts for his feeling as a victim of privately-run bus services in Shenzhen, where the hired conductor grabbed him and forcibly kidnapped him onto the bus (Example (42)).

(42) (Luke and Wei Zhang 2010: 175)

L: *en **la shangqu le ying la shangqu***
       'en dragged me onto the bus, forcibly dragged me up'

Apart from that, inserting can also do alignment work in Mandarin Chinese. In Example (43), the hosts of the Consumer Hotline express that they are on the side of a caller who complains against a shop being reluctant to take back a ring purchased there. According to Luke and Wei Zhang, the hosts defend the caller's consumer rights and express that they are on her/his side by inserting the deontic verb *yinggai* ('should') before *shi meiyou wenti* ('there's no problem'), which turns the statement 'It's not a problem' into 'It shouldn't be a problem' (2010: 169).

(43) (Luke and Wei Zhang 2010: 168)

S: *wo kan zhege **shi meiyou shenm- yinggai shi meiyou** wenti*
        'I think this is not- this shouldn't be a problem'

Inserting can also be used to do identity work in Mandarin Chinese: inserting words like *zanmen* 'us' or *tamen* 'them' may have the effect of reducing or increasing distance, respectively (Examples (44) and (45)).

(44) (Luke and Wei Zhang 2010: 171)

S: *natian wo zai **Gang-** zai **zanmen GangD**a de zhe-ge shudian qu mai shu*
        'the other day I was at the Hong- at our Hong Kong U bookshop buying some books.'

(45) (Luke and Wei Zhang 2010: 172)

S: *nabian hai **you xie- tamen you xie** shiqing xiang gen wo taolun taolun*
        'over there there are still some- they have some things that (they) want to discuss with me'

In Hungarian, it is also possible that, instead of correcting an apparent mistake, inserting is used solely to do interactional work. The corpus shows that the interactional function Lerner (2013: 105) suggests for turn-constructional delaying practices, i.e., expressing the speaker's unease about what s/he is about to say, can be applied not only for turn-constructional delaying practices, but also for inserting in Hungarian. According to my observations, this interactional function can appear, for example, during the delivery of criticism in the Hungarian corpus. This means that beyond replacing (Example (27)) and recycling (Examples (34), (35)), Hungarian speakers may also use inserting when they express a critical attitude towards a person or an institution. In Examples (46) and (47), the speakers reduce the power of their critical assessments by modifying talk through inserting. In Example (46), Anna, Bálint, and Gabi are discussing the situation of women who go to a job interview and plan to have a baby in the near future. Bálint criticises the companies which do not employ such women because of the future disadvantages that the women's maternity leave[16] would bring for their business.

(46) (bea008f006: 507)

01 B: *mélyen   felháborít   hogy   ö: hogy   ezt*
      deeply   incenses   that   u:h   that   this.ACC
      'I am deeply shocked at the situation that u:h that

02   *bármilyen   m:unkaadó   (.) mh   bármilyen   mértékben   ö:*
    any.kind   employer   um   any.kind   extent.INE   u:h
    any kind of employer (.) um to any degree u:h

03   ***f-   megpróbálja   figyelembe   venni   hogy   ö:***
    t-   PVB.tries.DEF   consideration.ILL   take.INF   that   u:h
    t- makes an attempt to take into consideration u:h

04   *hogy   ki(.)nek   mik   a   családalapítási*
    that   who.GEN   what.PL   the   family.starting.ADJDER
    who takes on what in connection with

05   *vállalásai*
    commitments.POSS.3SG
    starting a family'

B: I am deeply shocked at the situation that u:h that any kind of employer (.) um
    to any degree u:h **t- makes an attempt to take into consideration** u:h who
    takes on what in connection with starting a family

In line 01, Bálint starts critically by saying that it is shocking for him that companies take into consideration women's future plans for starting a family, i.e. having a baby. After the first sound in line 03, he breaks off (*f-* ('t-')), and inserts *megpróbálja* ('tries to', 'makes an attempt to') before *figyelembe venni* ('take into consideration'). This modification decreases the power of his critical remark and reduces his responsibility for it, since, instead of stating that the companies take into consideration the candidates' plans when deciding whether to employ them or not, he just says that the companies make an attempt to do that. This may also express Bálint's unease about producing criticism, which is supported by the hesitancy marker *ö:* ('u:h') before the inserting. This stretched hesitation marker cannot be regarded as the repair initiation of the inserting, because the inserting is initiated later, by a cut-off, after the speaker has started to pronounce *f*. For this reason, I argue that the use of *ö:* 'u:h' here is a repair operation with a delaying function expressing the speaker's unease when he is delivering criticism (see Section 5.2).

In Example (47), Ági, Zsuzsi, and Marcsi are talking about Hungarian television talent shows.

(47) (SZTEPSZI2: 790)

01 Á: *a   média   nem   föltétlenül   (.) **a**   (.)   **csak**   **a***
    the   media   not   necessarily   the   only   the
    'the media is not necessarily (.) guided **by** (.) **only by**

02   *jóindulat   v:ezérli.   hogy   majd   tehetséget   faragunk*
     goodwill   guides.DEF   that   then   talent.ACC   carve.1PL.INDEF
     goodwill. the intention of making a talent

03   *belő* [*le   hanem*   NEKI   EZ   A   HASZNOS   HOGY   =
     of.her/him   but   for.it   this   the   useful   that
     out of somebo[dy but FOR THEM IT IS THIS THAT IS USEFUL THAT]=

04 Zs: [*hát   nem.*
          DM[17]   not
          [they're not.

05 M: [*persze   hogy   nem.   sőt,   biztos   hogy   nem.*
          of.course   that   not   what.is.more   sure   that   not
          [of course, they're not. what is more, they're definitely not.

06 Á: =*hogy   esetleg*   ([   ])
     that   possibly
     =that   possibly   ([   ])

07 M: [*szerintem   semmi   más   csak*   ]   *a   pénz.*
                  I.think   nothing   else   only   the money
                  [in my opinion, nothing else but   ] money.

08 Á: *igen.*
     yes
     yes.

09 Zs: *csak   a   pénz.   ja.   (.)   azt   adják*
     only   the   money   yeah   that.ACC   broadcast.3PL.DEF
     only money. yeah. (.) they broadcast only the programmes

10   *le   amit   az   emberek   néznek.*
     PVB   what.ACC   the   people   watch.3PL.INDEF
     that people will watch.'

Á: the media is not necessarily (.) guided **by** (.) **only by** goodwill. the intention of making
    a talent out of somebo [dy but FOR THEM IT IS THIS THAT IS USEFUL THAT =
Zs: [they're not.
M: [of course, they're not. what is more, they're definitely not.
Á: =that possibly ([   ])
M: [in my opinion, nothing else but] money.
Á: yes.
Zs: only money. yeah. (.) they broadcast only the programmes that people will watch.

When, in line 01, Ági begins to give her opinion about what the aims of these pro-grammes can be, her turn-design projects that she is about to explain what is not the leading ethical principle of the Hungarian media (*a média nem föltétlenül (.) a* ('media is not necessarily (.) guided by')). After a short pause, however, she goes back to change the turn with the inserting of *csak* ('only'), which creates a conces-sive form: goodwill can be one (but not the only one) of the leading principles of the media (*a média nem föltétlenül (.) a (.) csak a jóindulat v:ezérli* 'media is not necessarily (.) guided by (.) only by goodwill'). In this way, the repair operation decreases the power of Ági's critical opinion and reduces her responsibility for it. The possibility that the self-repair also results from her unease about giving a critical opinion is supported by the two pauses in line 01, as well as by another interesting phenomenon; after the other co-participants agree with Ági, forming a much more radical opinion (i.e., that media is guided only by money), Ági joins them with a categorical 'yes' in line 08. This means that her earlier, milder opin-ion (downgraded by the use of the inserting) did not come from conviction, but rather from her unease about what she was about to say, as she was somewhat loath to deliver her criticism before knowing the others' opinions on the topic. This means that, similarly to the interactional function Lerner (2013) suggests for turn-constructional delaying practices, employing inserting during the delivery of criticism may also show that the speaker 'is somewhat loath to say' something, in other words, this means of delivery 'can be understood as a somewhat milder substitute for another, more accusatory formulation' (Lerner 2013: 104).

The last repair operation I will deal with in more detail in this book is aborting.

5.4 Aborting

In *aborting*, the speaker interrupts the ongoing turn-constructional unit and starts anew with another TCU (cf. Laakso and Sorjonen 2010: 1153). Schegloff (2013: 52) says that there are two possible orientations towards a TCU which is left uncompleted: the speaker may abandon what s/he has said altogether, or s/he may only abandon the way the turn has been done so far, in favour of another way of doing the same undertaking. I will regard only the second orientation as a repair operation, when the speaker starts the same action in a different form, with a different TCU. Laakso and Sorjonen (2010: 1157) note that, while inserting and replacing preserve the syntactic shape of the utterance (e.g., the type of the clause), abandoning leaves the syntactic construction altogether uncompleted. In Example (48) below, for example, where Péter tries to explain how the en-gine worked in old cars, he abandons his TCU-so-far (this point is indicated by a cut-off on the article in line 02) and restructures his description in a simpler way.

(48) (bea002f002: 77)

01	P:	*a*	*gázpedál*	*is*	*ö:*	*teljesen*	*mechanikus*
		the	accelerator	also	u:h	totally	mechanical

'**the accelerator also u:h in a totally mechanical**

02	*úton*	*került*	*kapcsolatba*	*a-*	*az*
	way.SUP	came	contact.ILL	the	that

way came into contact with the- there was

03	*porlasztós*	*volt*	*nem*	*befecskendezős*
	carburettor.ADJDER	was.3SG	not	fuel.injected

a carburettor not fuel injection'

P: **the accelerator also u:h in a totally mechanical way came into contact with the- there was a carburettor not fuel injection**

Aborting can also be used as a device for downgrading the force of the action. In Example (49), Ábel, Boglárka, and Linda are talking about the effects of marijuana. Since earlier in the conversation all of them say that they have not tried any kind of drugs, Ábel invokes his acquaintances' opinion, according to which, the effects of marijuana are similar to those of drinking alcohol. After a short discussion, Linda also invokes her acquaintances' opinions; the following example starts here.

(49) (SZTEPSZI8: 1067)

01	L:	*hát*	*nekem*	*akik*	*ö*	*ismerőseim*
		well	to.me	who.PL	uh	acquaintances.POSS.1SG

'**well my acquaintances who**

02	*mondták*	*ők*	*nem*	*nem*	*ezt*	*mondták*
	told.3PL.DEF	they	not	not	this.ACC	said.3PL.DEF

have told me this it's not it's not what they said

03	*hanem*	*inkább*	*azt*	*hogy-*	*vagy*	*több*	(.)
	but	rather	that.ACC	that	or	several	

but rather- or I have heard several (.)

04	*olyat*	*hallottam*	*hogy*	*mondjuk*	*szar*	*volt*
	such.ACC	heard.1SG.INDEF	that	so.to.say	shit	was.3SG

opinions that so to say it felt like shit

05	*vagy vagy rossz*	*volt*	[	*utána*	]
	or or bad	was.3SG		after.it	

or or it felt bad [after it]

06 Á: [*hát az   el*]*sőket   mindig*
                                        well the   first.PL.ACC   always
                                        [well they say that the first ones are always

07   *azt   mondják   hogy   szar.*
        that.ACC   say.3PL.DEF   that   shit
        shit.'

L: **well my acquaintances who have told me this it's not it's not what
    they said but rather- or I have heard several (.) opinions that so to
    say it felt like shit or or it felt bad [after it**
Á: [well they say that the first ones are always shit.

At first, Linda refers to all of her acquaintances who have told her about their experiences with using marijuana (*ők* ('they') in line 02), but in line 03 she initiates
an aborting repair with a cut-off and restricts the category of referents to 'several
opinions': *vagy több (.) olyat hallottam* ('or I have heard several (.) opinions'). In
this way she downgrades the force of the opinion she invokes, that is, that after
smoking a joint it feels worse than after drinking alcohol. This kind of repair
makes it possible for the speaker to take responsibility only for the restricted
category of referents, i.e., only for some opinions. In line 06, Ábel adds that the
first 'ones' (meaning the first joints) are always said to be bad. It is interesting to
observe that the words 'drug', 'marijuana' or 'joint' are nowhere to be found in the
example, which could be the result of the fact that all types of drugs are illegal in
Hungary: the speakers are talking about people who are their acquaintances and
involved in an illegal activity.

   Schegloff's English example below contains two aborting operations following one another (a1 and a2): the repair involves the double abandoning of the
TCU-in-progress, and two new efforts to carry out the same action.

(50) (Schegloff 2013: 53)

01   Shr: Who w's the girl that was outside
02   his door? the store?
03   (0.8)
04   Mrk: Debbie.
05   (0.8)
06   Shr: Who's Debbie.
07   Mrk: °Katz.
08   (0.7)
09   Mrk: –>a1 **She's jus' that girl thet: uh:, (0.2)**
10   –>a2 **.hh I met her through uh:m::, (1.0)**
11   I met 'er in <u>West</u>wood.=I caught that- (.)

12		'Member I wenttuh see the premie:r of (0.3)
13		Lost Horizon? [(
14	Shr:	[I DID'N KNOW YOU <u>did</u>,=

When Sherrie cannot identify who Debbie is in line 06, instead of the recognitional reference form which is designed for someone who already knows about the person who is referred to (line 04) (Sacks and Schegloff 1979), Mark tries to refer to the woman concerned in a different way. However, he abandons this effort in line 09 (a1) and launches another try in line 10. This time instead of using a recognitional descriptor, he tries to describe how he has met Debbie (through somebody). Then he abandons this effort as well, and instead of referring to the person through whom he met the girl, he refers to the place where he met her ('I met 'er in <u>West</u>wood'). Mark therefore produces three TCUs implementing the same action when explaining to Sherrie who Debbie is: 1) 'She's jus' that girl thet: uh:, (0.2)' (line 09), 2) '.hh I met her through uh:m::, (1.0)' (line 10), 3) 'I met 'er in <u>West</u>wood' (line 11), and he employs two aborting repairs (a1 and a2).

Now, I have introduced the four repair operations which are the focus of my research. Since recycling and replacing have been investigated in areally and typologically diverse languages by Fox et al. (2009) and Fox et al. (2010), I begin my comparative examination with them. Although the two repair operations have been examined in respect of the same factors[18] in both studies, the aim of these examinations was not to compare the two operations with each other. They focused rather on the relationship between the factors at issue both in the case of recycling and in the case of replacing. However, if we put together their results concerning recycling and those concerning replacing, we will suspect the possibility of some kind of relationship between the two repair operations. In Chapter 6, I aim to find out whether this suspicion is borne out.

First, in order to extend the cross-linguistic investigation of Fox et al. (2009) and Fox et al. (2010) to another language, I will examine Hungarian in respect of frequency, site of repair initiation, and the length and syntactic class of the target word[19] in recycling and replacing repairs. Then, in the light of these cross-linguistic examinations, I will consider the potential relationship between the two repair operations by finding connections between the results concerning recycling and the results concerning replacing, both in the previous literature and in my investigation.

CHAPTER 6

Recycling and replacing

6.1 Recycling and replacing in nine languages

Fox et al. (2009) examine the site of repair initiation in the case of recycling and replacing in seven languages: English, Bikol, Sochiapam Chinantec, Finnish, Indonesian, Japanese, and Mandarin. They involve the factors of site of initiation and the length and syntactic class of the target word in their research. After this cross-linguistic investigation, they argue that there is an underlying universal tendency in their seven languages to initiate recycling after and replacing before recognisable completion (the only exception is Japanese), but this pattern is sometimes masked by language-specific features (2009: 80). Taking into account word length and syntactic class, they find that both in recycling and replacing repairs monosyllabic words tend to be repaired after recognisable completion, and multisyllabic words tend to be repaired prior to recognisable completion (2009: 99). In the case of bisyllabic words, speakers do not tend to show any preference for site of initiation (2009: 100). In five of the seven languages investigated (English, Sochiapam Chinantec, Finnish, Indonesian, Mandarin), speakers range from moderately to highly more likely to initiate repair in a function word than a content word (2009: 97). The study by Fox et al. (2010) focuses on whether there is a relationship between the typological characteristics of English, German, and Hebrew and the appearance of recycling and replacing repairs in these languages. They find an over-representation of content words in replacing repairs and function words in recycling repairs in each of the three languages. As far as the Hungarian language is concerned, considering the lexical categories which serve as destinations of recycling in Hungarian, both Lerch's (2007) conversation analytic and Gyarmathy's (2009) psycholinguistic studies observe that the speakers of their Hungarian corpora tend to recycle back to function words rather than content words.

Although neither Fox et al. (2009) nor Fox et al. (2010) explore the frequencies of recycling and replacing in their corpora, their collections of self-repair instances contain many more recycling than replacing repairs in all the examined languages in both studies (cf. Fox et al. 2009: 63; Fox et al. 2010: 2490) (Table 6.1).

Table 6.1: The number of recycling and replacing instances in the collections of Fox et al. (2009) and Fox et al. (2010)[1]

	Recycling repair	Replacing repair
English	111	36
Hebrew	128	27
German	98	44
Indonesian	117	29
Sochiapam Chinantec	185	16
Japanese	147	53
Mandarin	115	35
Bikol	162	23
Finnish	116	46

[1] While the source of the English, Hebrew, and German results is Fox et al. 2010, the numbers of the repair operation instances in Indonesian, Sochiapam Chinantec, Japanese, Mandarin, Bikol, and Finnish come from the study by Fox et al. (2009).

On the basis of the research of Fox et al. (2009) and Fox et al. (2010) involving a total of nine languages in their examinations, it can be suggested that recycling is a more frequent repair operation than replacing in all the examined languages. In the next section I attempt to find out whether there is such a difference between the frequency of recycling and replacing in Hungarian. Following the methodology of Fox et al. (2009) and Fox et al. (2010), I examine recycling and replacing in Hungarian conversations relative to each other and compare my results with the previous findings concerning the other languages so far examined in this respect.

6.2 Recycling and replacing in Hungarian

6.2.1 Syntactic category and word length in Hungarian recycling repairs

The total number of self-repair instances examined in the first phase of the present research into Hungarian is 557, consisting of 415 recycling and 142 replacing repairs (Németh 2012: 2024). As far as the ratio of the number of recycling repairs to the number of replacing repairs is concerned, Hungarian shows the same pattern as the languages examined so far (see Table 6.1). Unlike the previous examinations, however, the present research takes into account all recycling and replacing self-repairs in eight conversations from the BEA database and two conversations from the SZTEPSZI corpus (17 speakers across ten everyday interactions in Hungarian, total length: 2 hours 25 minutes 4 seconds; see Chapter 4). Consequently, the present examination can be regarded as a frequency analysis. Following the cross-linguistic investigation by Fox et al. (2009) and Fox et al. (2010), I now explore the length and syntactic class of words in which the speakers of the Hungarian corpus tend to initiate recycling and replacing; i.e., I find out whether they tend to initiate recycling and replacing in monosyllabic, bisyllabic, or multisyllabic words, and function or content words, respectively. Then I try to reveal whether the type of the repair operation, the length of the target word, and/or the syntactic class of the target word influence the site of repair initiation in recycling and replacing repairs in Hungarian conversations. In order to see the relationship between the variables listed above, I will use 2×2 and 2×3 Pearson's chi-square statistics, and calculate the Cramér's V measure of nominal association. Using these methods of analysis, I intend to test how likely it is that the observed distributions are due to chance (Pearson's chi-square), and how strong the relationship is between the variables (Cramér's contingency coefficient). The null hypothesis of the chi-square test will always be that there is no relationship between the variables listed above. After observing the distribution of values on the separate variables, the test computes the expected conjoint distribution if there is no relationship between the variables. This expected distribution is then compared with the actual distribution of cases in the sample (Babbie 2010: 483). The obtained chi-square value shows the overall discrepancy between the expected and the actually discovered conjoint distribution of values. The higher the obtained chi-square value is, the less likely it is that there is no relationship between the variables (Babbie 2010: 484). In the analyses below, in each case an asterisk will indicate the significant chi-square values. Where the result of the test is significant, I will check whether the different variables equally contribute to this result or whether the significance comes entirely from certain rows or columns. I will do this analysis by using chi-square goodness-of-fit tests. I will supplement the chi-square statistics with the Cramér's V measure of nominal association that provides a measurement of how strong the association between the variables is. The Cramér's V statistics range from 0 to 1. Higher Cramér's V values indicate stronger associations (Cramér 1999 [1946]). I will also check whether the frequencies of the word-length and syntactic class categories observed in recycling and replacing repairs follow from their overall frequencies in the corpus. For this reason, I have coded the corpus not only for the syntactic category, length, and site of initiation of the words involved in recycling and replacing, but also for the syntactic category and length of all words in the corpus.

I first explore how word length and syntactic class influence the execution of recycling repair in the Hungarian corpus. Tables 6.2a and 6.2b, and Figures 6.1 and 6.2 display the distribution of repair types (recycling and replacing) by syntactic class and word length in the corpus. We can see that the result of the chi-square test is significant in both cases. If there were no relationship between the variables, the probability that we obtain a chi-square value of this magnitude in both cases would be less than 1%. Consequently, we have to assign a high plausibility value to the statement that there is a relationship both between the type of the repair operation and the syntactic class of the target word, and between the type of the repair operation and the length of the target word in the corpus.

Table 6.2a: Observed frequencies of recycling and replacing repairs by syntactic class (Németh 2012: 2025, Table 1a)

	Destination of recycling	Replaced item	Total
Function words	315 (76%)	48 (34%)	363
Content words	100 (24%)	94 (66%)	194
Total	415	142	557

$\chi^2(1) = 82.61^*$, $p < .01$; Cramér's V = .385* (very strong association between the two variables), $p < .01$

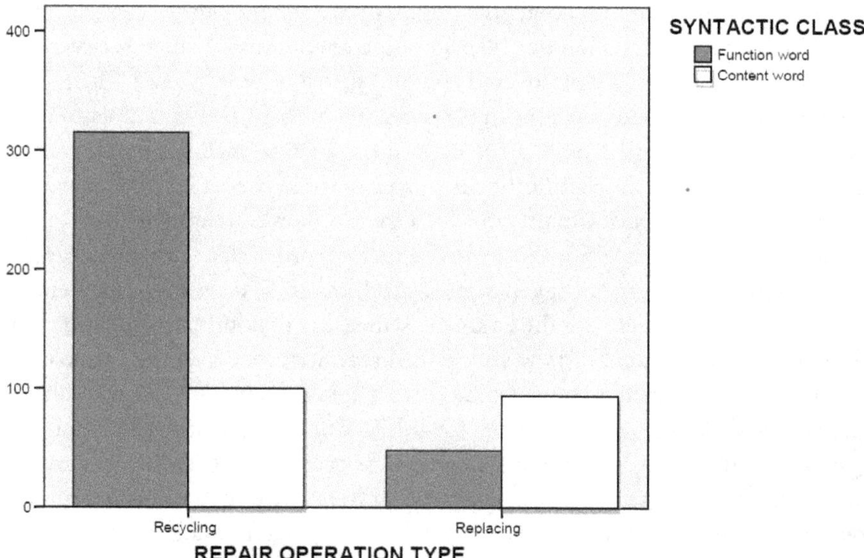

Figure 6.1: Observed frequencies of recycling and replacing repairs by syntactic class

Table 6.2b: Observed frequencies of recycling and replacing repairs by word length (Németh 2012: 2025, Table 1b)

	Destination of recycling	Replaced item	Total
Monosyllabic words	304 (73%)	50 (35%)	354
Bisyllabic words	75 (18%)	32 (23%)	107
Multisyllabic words	36 (9%)	60 (42%)	96
Total	415	142	557

Monosyllabic/Bisyllabic/Multisyllabic: $\chi^2(2) = 94.40^*$, $p < .01$

Cramér's V = .411* (strong association between the variables), $p < .01$

Let us consider recycling and replacing separately. Tables 6.2a and 6.2b show that the speakers of the Hungarian corpus recycle back most frequently to function words (cf. Lerch 2007; Gyarmathy 2009) and monosyllabic words (see Examples (33)–(36) in Section 5.2). First, let us consider syntactic categories. The result of the chi-square goodness-of-fit test for the distribution of recycling instances with respect to syntactic class is significant: $\chi^2(1) = 111.38^*$, $p < .01$. This means that the distribution of this repair type across syntactic class is not random. Although function words make up 76% of all destinations of recycling compared with 24% for content words, in order to be sure that this difference does not derive from the relative frequencies of the two syntactic categories in the corpus, we have to

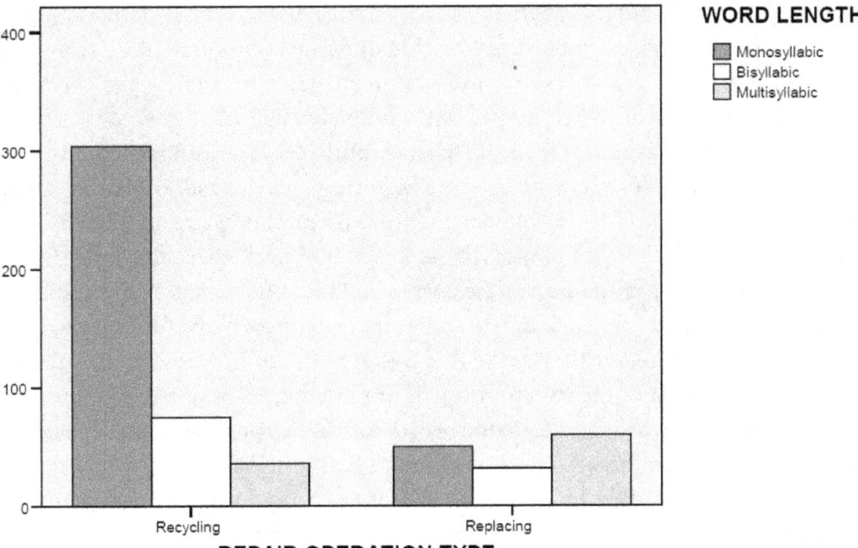

Figure 6.2: Observed frequencies of recycling and replacing repairs by word length

consider our result in relation to the whole corpus. Table 6.3 provides the figures for the syntactic class and word length of all words in the corpus.

Table 6.3: Observed frequencies of words by word length and syntactic class in the corpus (Németh 2012: 2026, Table 2)

	Function words	Content words	Total
Monosyllabic words	7,377	2,884	10,261 (46%)
Bisyllabic words	1,995	4,815	6,810 (31%)
Multisyllabic words	209	4,899	5,108 (23%)
Total	9,581 (43%)	12,598 (57%)	22,179

The corpus contains 9,581 function words (43%) and 12,598 content words (57%). In Table 6.2a we have seen that in recycling repairs the function to content word ratio is 76% to 24%. Since in the whole corpus there are more content words than function words, the frequency of function words in recycling repairs cannot follow from their frequency in the corpus. If we turn to word length, Table 6.2b shows that the most common destinations of recycling repairs in the Hungarian corpus are monosyllabic words. Monosyllabic words make up 73% of all destinations of recycling compared with 18% to bisyllabic and 9% to multisyllabic words. The result of the chi-square goodness-of-fit test for the distribution of recycling instances with respect to word length is significant, i.e., the distribution is not random: monosyllabic/bisyllabic/multisyllabic: $\chi^2(2) = 303.09^*$, $p < . 01$. Again, to be sure that this difference does not come from the relative frequencies of the three word-length categories in the corpus, we have to consider this result in relation to the whole corpus (Table 6.3): 46% of the words are monosyllabic, 31% are bisyllabic, and 23% are multisyllabic in the corpus. This ratio does not justify such a high frequency of monosyllabic words in recycling repairs (73% of all destinations of recycling are monosyllabic). Therefore, the frequency of monosyllabic words in recycling repairs is not likely to follow from their frequency in the corpus, either. This means that the speakers of the corpus recycle back most frequently to monosyllabic function words. Here we can ask whether they make this frequent use of monosyllabic function words because most of the function words are monosyllabic or because most of the monosyllabic words are function words in the corpus? To see this clearly, we have to compare the occurrence of monosyllabic and function words in the whole corpus. According to Table 6.3, 77% of the function words are monosyllabic (9,581 function words; 7,377 monosyllabic function words) and 72% of the monosyllabic words are function words in the corpus (10,261 monosyllabic words; 7,377 monosyllabic function words). This suggests that the reason for the high frequency of monosyllabic function words in recycling repairs is that most of the function words are monosyllabic, rather than our other observation, namely, that most of the monosyllabic words are function words in the corpus. Thus, as Jurafsky et al. (1998) observed in the case of English, high-frequency function words are often phonologically reduced in Hungarian as well, and this can explain the high frequency of monosyllabic function words as the destinations of recycling in the corpus. In other words, when the speakers of the Hungarian corpus recycle back to monosyllabic function words, syntactic class plays a more important role than word length.

Let us examine word-length categories separately. Tables 6.4a–c below display the three word-length categories with the corresponding figures from the whole corpus.

Table 6.4a: **Observed frequencies** of monosyllabic words in recycling repairs and the corpus (Németh 2012: 2026, Table 3a)

	Destination of recycling	**Whole corpus**
Function words	265 (87%)	7,377 (72%)
Content words	39 (13%)	2,884 (28%)

Table 6.4b: **Observed frequencies** of bisyllabic words in recycling repairs and the corpus (Németh 2012: 2026, Table 3b)

	Destination of recycling	**Whole corpus**
Function words	47 (63%)	1,995 (29%)
Content words	28 (37%)	4,815 (71%)

Table 6.4c: **Observed frequencies** of multisyllabic words in recycling repairs and the corpus (Németh 2012: 2026, Table 3c)

	Destination of recycling	**Whole corpus**
Function words	3 (8%)	209 (4%)
Content words	33 (92%)	4,899 (96%)

Table 6.4a shows that taking into consideration the whole corpus, the frequency of monosyllabic function words is much higher than the frequency of monosyllabic content words (72%–28%). However, in recycling repairs we find an even bigger difference between the two syntactic class categories (87%–13%),

which signals the privileged status of function words among monosyllabic words serving as destinations for recycling repairs. The group of bisyllabic words is the only word-length category where the figures for recycling repairs are in inverse proportion to the same figures for the whole corpus (Table 6.4b). Although there are more bisyllabic content words than bisyllabic function words in the corpus (71%–29%), in recycling repairs we can find more bisyllabic function words than bisyllabic content words (63%–37%). As far as multisyllabic words are concerned, in the whole corpus there are many more multisyllabic content words than multisyllabic function words (96%–4%). Although in recycling repairs there are still many more multisyllabic content words than multisyllabic function words (92%–8%), this difference is not so sharp as in the whole corpus, which, together with the other word-length category results, supports the privileged status of function words in recycling repair in the Hungarian corpus.

These results are in accordance with Lerch's (2007) and Gyarmathy's (2009) previous findings concerning Hungarian, and the results of Fox et al. (2010) concerning Hebrew, English, and German. Fox and her colleagues point out that all three languages have function words which precede the content words they serve as adjuncts to (e.g., prepositions or determiners), and in all three languages there is a tendency to recycle back to function words rather than content words. On the basis of these observations, they predict that languages with function words preceding their respective content words (which they think are mainly verb-initial and verb-medial languages) will show a preference for recycling back to function words rather than content words (Fox et al. 2010: 2504). This is also supported by earlier studies (Fox et al. 1996; Rieger 2003; Lerch 2007; Gyarmathy 2009; Fox et al. 2009), among which Fox et al. (1996: 205) note that in the languages where speakers have no function words preceding nouns (e.g., the postpositional Japanese), speakers do not use this strategy. Fox et al. (2010) also suggest that function words may be recycled to delay the next content word due, and therefore are likely to be used as the destinations of recycling (2010: 2502). Fox et al. (2009: 97) also claim that the recycling of function words is an extremely useful device for the speaker to delay the next content word due. Lerch (2007) considers the lexical categories serving as destinations for recycling in Hungarian. She observes that the speakers of her Hungarian corpus tend to recycle back to function words, and they employ recycling to delay the next lexical element due (Lerch 2007: 127). Since the phrase-beginning elements tend to be function words in Hungarian, there are several function words preceding content words in the language. While definite and indefinite articles, or demonstrative determiners together with the definite article project an upcoming noun phrase, conjunctions and relative pronouns occur at the beginning of clauses (Lerch 2007: 127) (see the recycling in Example (33) repeated here as Example (51)).

(51) (bea007f005: 430)

```
01  F:  akkor   azt          mondta        hogy    hogy    hogy    (.) hogy
        then    that.ACC     told.3SG.DEF  that    that    that        that
        'then he told that that that (.) that

02      tetszettek              (.)    nekik
        were.pleasing.3PL              to.them
        they liked (.) them (the lessons)'
```

The present examination thus also supports Fox et al.'s (2010: 2504) prediction: my results show that the speakers of my Hungarian corpus tend to recycle back to function words. All these findings illuminate how the methods of repair are shaped by the linguistic resources of the language in question and therefore draw our attention to the close relationship between grammar and repair.

All the explanations listed above for the over-representation of function words in recycling repair imply that in conversations, speakers may find it necessary to delay content words rather than function words. What can be the motive for this? Fox et al. (2009: 103) remark that content words are open class, hence there are a larger number of potential candidates among them in any given context than there are for function words. They also note that content words are usually of lower frequency than function words, and the interactants face a greater challenge in selecting the appropriate word (Fox et al. 2009: 103). This claim can serve as a potential answer to our question: speakers may find it necessary to delay content words because they face a greater challenge in selecting the appropriate content word as opposed to the selection of appropriate function words. Selecting content words can thus demand more time than selecting function words. Furthermore, in the cases when recycling is used at the emergence of overlapping talk, and it serves as a device for delaying the talk that follows in order to get it said in the clear, it can be assumed that speakers tend to avoid the possible compromised hearing of content words and delay content words rather than function words. That is, for the above reasons, content words may be more difficult to infer if they are not produced in the clear (see Example (32) in Section 5.2). Finally, the interactional function Lerner (2013: 105) suggests for turn-constructional delaying strategies, namely, the function of delaying a projectably delicate term, also supports the idea that speakers tend to delay content words rather than function words: it can be assumed that delicate terms are rather content words (see Section 5.2).

In this section I have found that the speakers of the Hungarian corpus tend to recycle back to monosyllabic function words, and in the recycling repairs of the corpus, syntactic class plays a more important role than word length. In the next section, I examine replacing repair in the Hungarian corpus regarding the same features.

6.2.2 Syntactic category and word length in Hungarian replacing repairs

If we look at Table 6.2a and Figure 6.1 again (repeated below as Table 6.5 and Figure 6.3 for the sake of convenience), we can realise that the speakers of the Hungarian corpus employ content words in replacing repairs nearly twice as frequently as function words (66%–34%). The result of the chi-square goodness-of-fit test for the distribution of replacing instances with respect to syntactic class is significant: $\chi^2(1) = 14.90^*$, $p < .01$ (the distribution is not random). Let us consider this ratio in relation to the whole corpus again (see Table 6.3, repeated below as Table 6.6). We can see that the corpus contains 12,598 content words (57%) and 9,581 function words (43%). Table 6.5 shows that in replacing repairs the content to function word ratio is 66% to 34%. This difference is greater than the content to function word ratio in the whole corpus, which suggests that content words have a privileged status in replacing repairs (see the replacing in Example (26) repeated here as Example (52)).

Table 6.5: Observed frequencies of repair types by syntactic class (Németh 2012: 2025, Table 1a)

	Destination of recycling	Replaced item	Total
Function words	315 (76%)	48 (34%)	363
Content words	100 (24%)	94 (66%)	194
Total	415	142	557

$\chi^2(1) = 82.61^*$, $p < .01$; Cramér's V = .385* (very strong association between the two variables), $p < .01$

Table 6.6: Observed frequencies of words by word length and syntactic class in the corpus (Németh 2012: 2026, Table 2)

	Function words	Content words	Total
Monosyllabic words	7,377	2,884	10,261 (46%)
Bisyllabic words	1,995	4,815	6,810 (31%)
Multisyllabic words	209	4,899	5,108 (23%)
Total	9,581 (43%)	12,598 (57%)	22,179

(52) (SZTEPSZI2: 953)

```
01  G:  de      hogy    egy   egy   poén   kedvéért      fölál-   ö
        but     that    a     a     joke   for.the.sake  sacri-   uh
        'but for a a joke do you sacri- uh
```

```
02      kockára     teszed           egyébként    a:?
        cube.SUB    put.2SG.DEF      by.the.way   the
        risk, by the way, your (place at the university)?'
```

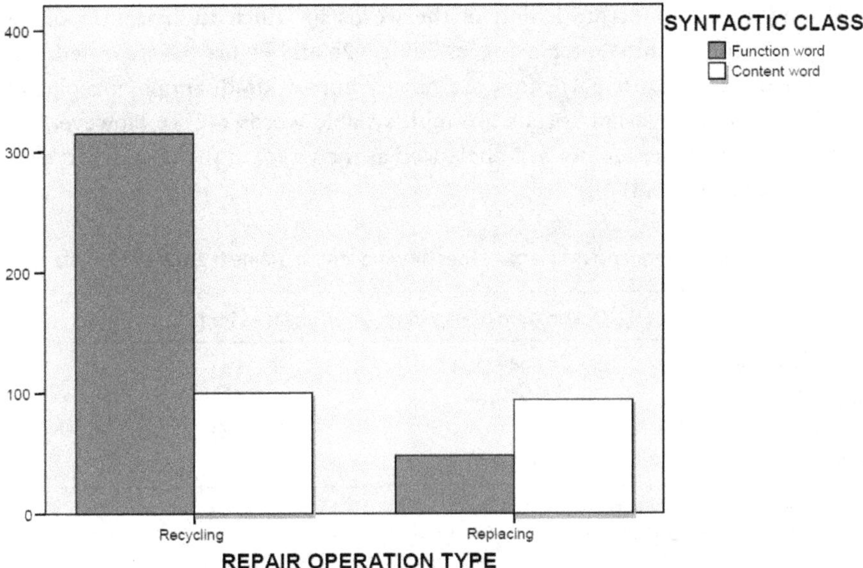

Figure 6.3: Observed frequencies of repair types by syntactic class

These results support the findings of the previous research on replacing in the conversation analytic literature. As was noted earlier, Fox et al. (2010: 2487) emphasise that the speakers of all their three languages replace content words at a disproportionately high rate. As a possible explanation, they note that content words may need to be replaced because they are inapposite (2010: 2503). Focusing on English, Fox et al. (2009: 76) also suggest that English speakers may employ replacing in cases where an inappropriate pronunciation or word has been produced. Why are content words more likely to be inapposite or inappropriate than function words? Here we can use exactly the same arguments as we used when explaining the necessity of delaying content words in the previous section: on the one hand, content words are open class, hence the number of potential candidates among them is higher in any given context than the number of candidates among function words (Fox et al. 2009: 103). On the other hand, content words are usually of lower frequency than function words, which means that the speaker faces a greater challenge when trying to select the appropriate term (Fox et al. 2009: 103). If the selection of appropriate content words represents a greater challenge for speakers than the selection of appropriate function words, we can also assume that when producing a content word, speakers are more likely to face problems which can lead to the need for a replacing than during the production of function words.

Taking into account the length of the words in which the speakers of the Hungarian corpus initiate replacing, as Table 6.2b and Figure 6.2 (repeated here as Table 6.7 and Figure 6.4) show, the most common destinations of replacing repairs in the Hungarian corpus are multisyllabic words (42%). However, the observed frequencies are not as unbalanced as they were in the case of recycling repairs (see Figure 6.4).

Table 6.7: Observed frequencies of repair types by word length (Németh 2012: 2025, Table 1b)

	Destination of recycling	Replaced item	Total
Monosyllabic words	304 (73%)	50 (35%)	354
Bisyllabic words	75 (18%)	32 (23%)	107
Multisyllabic words	36 (9%)	60 (42%)	96
Total	415	142	557

Monosyllabic/Bisyllabic/Multisyllabic: $\chi^2(2) = 94.40^*$, $p < .01$
Cramér's V $= .411^*$ (strong association between the variables), $p < .01$

The chi-square goodness-of-fit test for the distribution of replacing instances with respect to word length is significant (monosyllabic/bisyllabic/multisyllabic: $\chi^2(2) = 8.50^*$, $p < .05$). As the second column of Table 6.7 shows, although the most common replaced items are multisyllabic words, monosyllabic words are

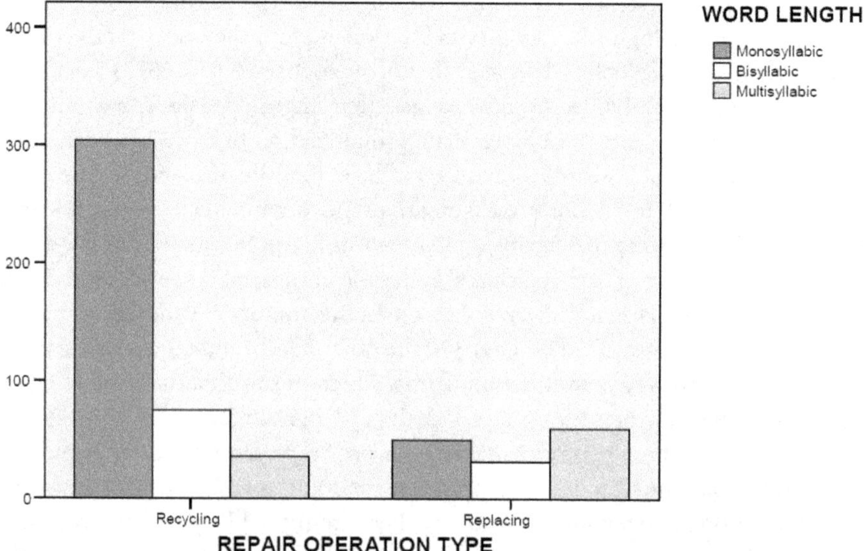

Figure 6.4: Observed frequencies of repair types by word length

also replaced at a relatively high rate by the speakers of the corpus. To find a possible explanation for this, let us include syntactic class in the examination.

Table 6.8a: Observed frequencies of monosyllabic words in replacing repairs and the corpus (Németh 2012: 2028, Table 6a)

	Replacing repairs	**Whole corpus**
Function words	37 (74%)	7,377 (72%)
Content words	13 (26%)	2,884 (28%)

Table 6.8b: Observed frequencies of bisyllabic words in replacing repairs and the corpus (Németh 2012: 2028, Table 6b)

	Replacing repairs	**Whole corpus**
Function words	9 (28%)	1,995 (29%)
Content words	23 (72%)	4,815 (71%)

Table 6.8c: Observed frequencies of multisyllabic words in replacing repairs and the corpus (Németh 2012: 2028, Table 6c)

	Replacing repairs	**Whole corpus**
Function words	2 (3%)	209 (4%)
Content words	58 (97%)	4,899 (96%)

Although the speakers of the Hungarian corpus replace content words at a higher rate than function words, this difference does not appear in the case of monosyllabic words (Table 6.8a). This result may follow from the over-representation of function words among monosyllabic words (the function to content word ratio is 72% to 28% in monosyllabic words), and the usage of the Hungarian definite article also contributes to this. That is to say, the Hungarian definite article has two alternants. *A* is used before words beginning with consonants and *az* before vowels. The article is used for delaying its respective noun phrase in 51 cases in the corpus. In 36 cases the article is recycled. However, since the speaker may employ the delay strategy because s/he does not know yet which noun to select (i.e., whether it will start with a consonant or a vowel), it can happen that s/he has to substitute *a* with *az*. The replacing of *a* with *az* occurs 15 times in the corpus (this represents 40% of the monosyllabic function word replacing repairs) (see Example (53)).

(53) (SZTEPSZI3: 853)

01 B: *ez   akkor **a:**   **az**   életkoromnak   így   nagyon
        this then   the   the   age.POSS.1SG.GEN   in.this.way   very
        'then this was a very

02   *megfelelő:*   *stratégiája*   *volt*
        appropriate   strategy.POSS.3SG   was.3SG
        appropriate strategy for my age'

Table 6.8c shows that multisyllabic content words are the most frequently re-placed words in the corpus. Here, the question is raised again: when the speakers of the Hungarian corpus replace multisyllabic content words, does word length or syntactic class play the key role? If we compare the occurrence of multisyllabic and content words in the whole corpus, we can see that 39% of the content words are multisyllabic (12,598 content words; 4,899 multisyllabic content words) and 96% of the multisyllabic words are content words in the corpus (5,108 multi-syllabic words; 4,899 multisyllabic content words) (Table 6.6). This suggests that the reason for the high frequency of multisyllabic content words in replacing re-pairs is that most of the multisyllabic words are content words in the Hungarian corpus. Thus, when the speakers of the Hungarian corpus replace multisyllabic content words, word length plays a more important role than syntactic class (see Example (52)).

Taking into account the difference between bi- and multisyllabic words, we find that the two word-length categories differ from monosyllabic words in that there are more content words than function words replaced in both categories (Tables 6.8b, 6.8c). While the bisyllabic function to content word ratio is 28% to 72% in replacing repairs, the same ratio is 3% to 97% in multisyllabic words. This means that the speakers of the Hungarian corpus replace multisyllabic content words at a higher rate than bisyllabic content words. This difference between bisyllabic and multisyllabic content words in replacing repairs could only be explained by the frequency of content words in the repair type if there were more content words among multisyllabic words than among bisyllabic words in the corpus. However, according to Tables 6.8b and 6.8c, there are 4,815 bisyllabic content words and 4,899 multisyllabic content words in the corpus. The numbers are nearly the same, which means that the different representations of bisyllabic and multisyl-labic words in replacing repair cannot really be explained by anything else but the fact that multisyllabic words are longer than bisyllabic ones.

All these observations suggest that in the Hungarian corpus, longer words are more likely to be replaced than shorter ones. What can be the reason for this? If we concentrate on the observation by Fox et al. (2009: 76), namely, that English speakers may employ replacing in cases where they have produced an inappropriate pronunciation or word, it can be assumed that in the case of longer words inappropriate pronunciation is more likely to occur than in the case of shorter words. My finding that in the replacing of multisyllabic content words word length plays a more important role than syntactic class in the Hungarian corpus may be due to the rich system of inflectional and derivational morphology in the language[1] (cf. Lerch 2007: 127).

In this section, I have found that the speakers of the Hungarian corpus tend to replace multisyllabic content words, and in replacing repair word length plays a more important role than syntactic class. Following the cross-linguistic examination of Fox et al. (2009), in the next section I try to reveal whether the type of the repair operation, the length of the target word, and/or the syntactic class of the target word influence the site of repair initiation, i.e., the location in the target word where speakers initiate repair in the Hungarian corpus.

6.2.3 The site of repair initiation and repair type in Hungarian

As for repair types and site of initiation in the Hungarian corpus, in Table 6.9 and Figure 6.5 we can see that while 61% of all replacing repairs are initiated before the word is recognisably complete, with recycling repairs this only occurs in 17% of cases. Conversely, 83% of all simple recycling repairs are initiated after recognisable completion, but with replacing repairs the figure is only 39%. The result of the chi-square test is significant. Again, if there were no relationship between the variables, the probability that we obtain a chi-square value of this magnitude would be less than 1%. Consequently, we have to assign a high plausibility value to the statement that there is a relationship between the variables. The value of Cramér's V also shows a strong association between site of initiation and repair type in the Hungarian corpus. The results of the chi-square goodness-of-fit tests for the distribution of repair types with respect to repair initiation are also significant; in other words, neither the distribution of recycling nor the distribution of replacing repairs are random across repair initiation type (recycling: $\chi^2(1) = 184.88^*$, $p < .01$; replacing: $\chi^2(1) = 6.33^*$, $p < .05$).

Table 6.9: Recognisable completion and repair operation types in the Hungarian corpus (Németh 2012: 2031, Table 10)

	Not recognisably complete	Recognisably complete	Total
Recycling	69 (17%)	346 (83%)	415
Replacing	86 (61%)	56 (39%)	142
Total	155 (28%)	402 (72%)	557

$\chi^2(1) = 101.69^*$, $p < .01$; Cramér's V = .427* (very strong association between the two variables), $p < .01$

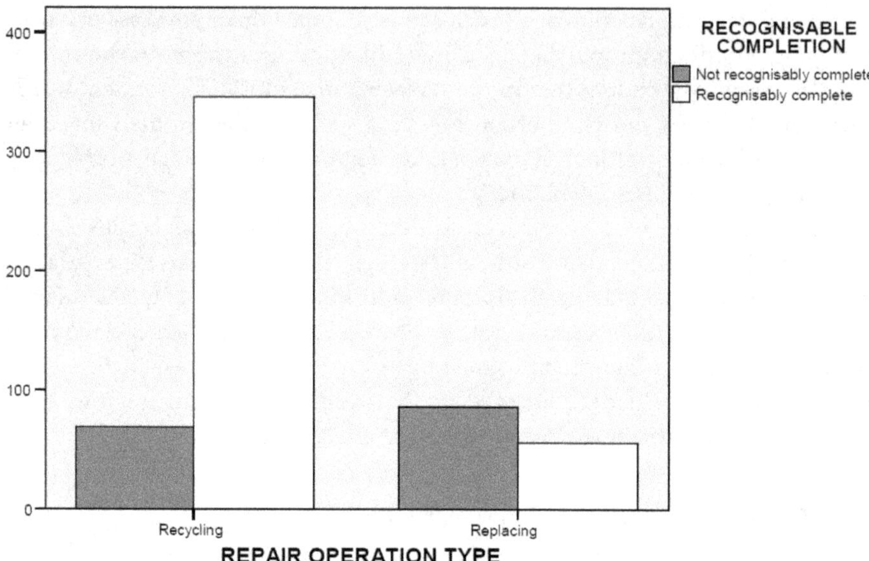

Figure 6.5: Recognisable completion and repair operation types in the Hungarian corpus

These results also support the cross-linguistic findings presented by Fox et al. (2009). Based on Jasperson's (1998) notions, Fox and her colleagues (2009: 74) suggest that repair initiation before recognisable completion is associated with repairs that change the preceding talk, i.e., have a retrospective orientation. The cross-linguistic results are in accordance with this prediction: replacing changes the preceding talk, i.e., has a retrospective orientation, and there is an underlying universal tendency in the languages examined so far to initiate replacing prior to recognisable completion. Fox et al. (2009: 80) propose that by using this strategy speakers may reduce accountability for inappropriate words. However, if we take into consideration the interactional aims described in the literature in connection with replacing repair, we can appreciate that, although the repair type always has a retrospective orientation, not all of its interactional functions support initiation before recognisable completion. While repair initiation in replacing can usually be associated with the speaker's accountability for the repairable, this account-ability does not imply that the speaker is unwilling to take responsibility. It can happen that the speaker takes responsibility for the replaced item (Fox et al. 2009: 102). It can also happen that although the speaker wants to make the replaced segment recognisable, s/he still does not take responsibility for its production. This is Jefferson's interactional situation described in Section 5.1. Jefferson (1974: 193) suggests that replacing a word with another, if the replaced segment is not recognisably complete but still recognisable, allows the speaker to produce an inappropriate word without being interactionally accountable for it. This case also supports initiation before recognisable completion in replacing repairs. The Hungarian results fit the pattern Fox et al. (2009) propose: replacing tends to be initiated before recognisable completion.

Continuing their train of thought, Fox and her colleagues argue that repair initiation after recognisable completion is associated with repairs that operate on the talk that follows, e.g., by delaying the next item due (2009: 74). Here, let us recall our argumentation for the repair operation status of recycling when it is employed solely to delay the talk that follows (see Section 5.2). If the speaker employs recycling as a device for delaying the next item due, and s/he does this in order to attend to possible trouble in speaking, hearing, or understanding the talk, then we should regard recycling as a repair operation. Nevertheless, as was noted in the argumentation at issue, when we analyse the particular occurrences of recycling in conversations, sometimes it can be difficult to identify their delaying function. In these cases, the analysis of other features of the phenomenon may help us to decide whether we face a delaying function or not. For example, if we take into consideration the site of repair initiation in these occurrences of recycling, repair initiation carried out after the word is recognisably complete supports a potential delaying function. According to the proposal of Fox et al. (2009: 80), the reason for the tendency to late repair initiation in the case of recycling is that it is frequently used to delay the next content word due. The Hungarian examination supports this statement: the observation that recycling tends to be initiated after recognisable completion may indicate that it is frequently employed to delay the next content word due in Hungarian conversations.

All in all, we can see that Hungarian fits the patterns suggested as universal: while recycling tends to be initiated after recognisable completion, replacing is generally initiated before the word is recognisably complete. However, the cross-linguistic investigation by Fox et al. (2009) shows that the patterns regarded as universal are often masked by language-specific features. Thus, it is plausible that there is a tendency to initiate recycling after and replacing before recognisable completion, but this pattern can be manifested in various ways in different languages. In Japanese, speakers tend towards initiation before the word is recognisably complete in both repair operation types. In Mandarin and Sochiapam Chinantec, speakers favour initiation after recognisable completion for both types of repair operation. In Bikol, speakers do not prefer either type of initiation. In English and Indonesian, the universal pattern assumed by Fox et al. (2009) appears to be uncovered: recycling tends to be initiated after the word is recognisably complete and replacing is mainly initiated before recognisable completion. Finally, Finnish speakers favour initiation before recognisable completion for replacing repairs and do not show any preference as to the site of repair initiation in recycling repairs (Fox et al. 2009: 79–80). One possible explanation for this diversity is the role of other factors beyond the functions of repair operation types, such as word length and syntactic class.

6.2.4 The site of repair initiation, word length, and syntactic class in Hungarian

Taking into account word length and syntactic class, Fox et al. (2009: 99) find that both recycling and replacing tend to be initiated after recognisable completion in monosyllabic words and prior to recognisable completion in multisyllabic words. In the case of bisyllabic words, speakers do not show any preference for a single site of initiation. The consequence of this is as follows: in languages in which speakers tend to initiate repair in monosyllabic words (e.g., Sochiapam Chinantec, Mandarin, and English), they usually initiate repair after recognisable completion, while in languages in which speakers initiate repair mainly in multisyllabic words (e.g., Japanese), they prefer initiation prior to recognisable completion. However, in languages where speakers do not show any preference as to the length of the words they initiate repair in, they will not show any preference for a single site of initiation, either (Fox et al. 2009: 100).

Let us see whether the syntactic class and/or the length of the target word influence the site of repair initiation in Hungarian conversations. So far we have seen that the speakers of the Hungarian corpus tend to use mainly monosyllabic function words as the destinations of recycling (see Examples (33)–(36) in Section 5.2), while they prefer multisyllabic content words in replacing repairs (see Example (52)). If we consider the suggestion of Fox et al. (2009) explicated above, namely, that the function of a repair operation has a pronounced effect on the site of initiation, we have to assume that in content and multisyllabic words speakers will tend to initiate repair before the word is recognisably complete, and they will tend to initiate repair after recognisable completion in function and monosyllabic words. The results of the statistical analyses carried out on the figures in Tables 6.10 and 6.11 meet our expectations. The results of the chi-square tests show an association both between site of initiation and syntactic class (Table 6.10, Figure 6.6), and between site of initiation and word length in the Hungarian corpus (Table 6.11, Figure 6.7). The results of the chi-square goodness-of-fit tests for the distribution of the certain syntactic class and word-length categories with respect to repair initiation are the following:

- function words: $\chi^2(1) = 252.91^*$, $p < .01$;
- content words: $\chi^2(1) = 16.16^*$, $p < .01$;
- monosyllabic words: $\chi^2(1) = 264.50^*$, $p < .01$;
- bisyllabic words: $\chi^2(1) = .75$, $p > .05$ → not significant;
- multisyllabic words: $\chi^2(1) = 48.16^*$, $p < .01$.

The only word-length category where the result of the test is not significant is the category of bisyllabic words. Here the speakers of the Hungarian corpus show no preference for site of initiation.

Table 6.10: Recognisable completion and syntactic class (Németh 2012: 2031, Table 11)

	Not recognisably complete	Recognisably complete	Total
Function words	30 (8%)	333 (92%)	363
Content words	125 (64%)	69 (36%)	194
Total	155 (28%)	402 (72%)	557

$\chi^2(1) = 198.60^*$, $p < .01$; Cramér's V = .597* (very strong association between the two variables), $p < .01$

Table 6.11: Recognisable completion and word length (Németh 2012: 2031, Table 12)

	Not recognisably complete	Recognisably complete	Total
Monosyllabic words	24 (7%)	330 (93%)	354
Bisyllabic words	49 (46%)	58 (54%)	107
Multisyllabic words	82 (85%)	14 (15%)	96
Total	155 (28%)	402 (72%)	557

Monosyllabic/Bisyllabic/Multisyllabic: $\chi^2(2) = 253.81^*$, $p < .01$
Cramér's V = .675* (strong association between the two variables), $p < .01$

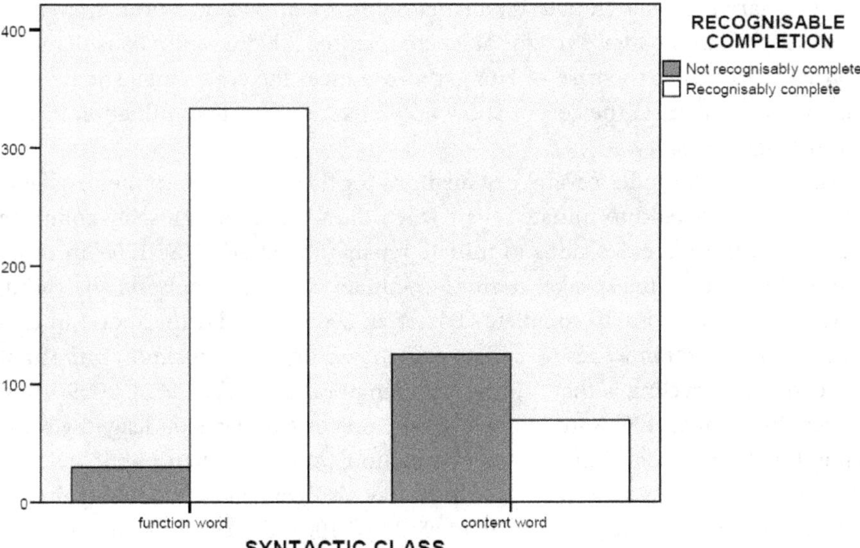

Figure 6.6: Recognisable completion and syntactic class

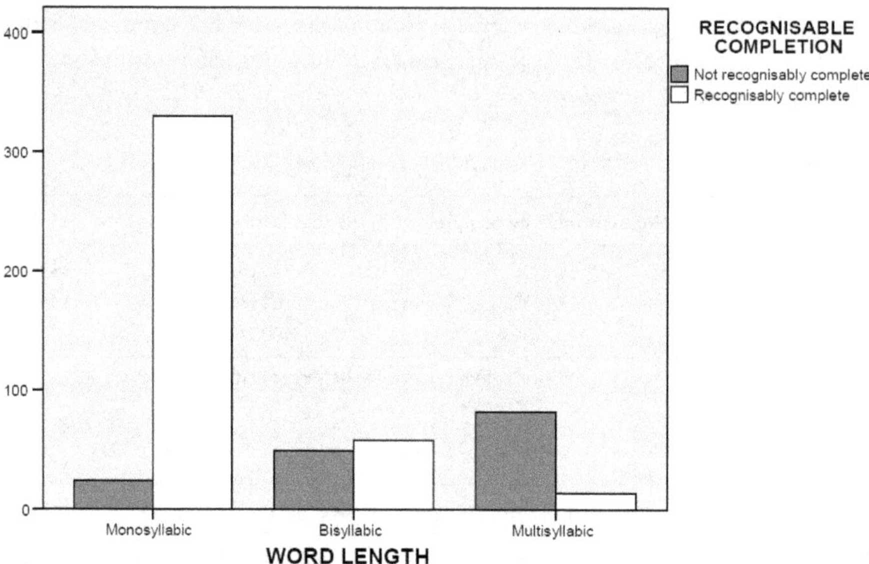

Figure 6.7: Recognisable completion and word length

These results also fit Fox et al.'s (2009: 100) prediction relating to word length: in languages in which speakers tend to initiate repair in monosyllabic words, they usually initiate repair after recognisable completion. As the speakers of the Hungarian corpus initiate repair mainly in monosyllabic words, they tend towards initiation after recognisable completion. Taking into consideration bisyllabic words, in the case of Hungarian we meet the cross-linguistic pattern again: the speakers of the corpus show no preference for site of initiation in this word-length category.

Fox et al. (2009) offer several explanations for these findings. In monosyllabic words, speakers tend to initiate repair when the word is recognisably complete because of their late decisions to initiate repair (Fox et al. 2009: 100); in other words, by the time the speaker decides to initiate repair in a monosyllabic word, it is already recognisably complete (Fox et al. 2009: 100). Furthermore, in languages with function words preceding content words, one of the most important functions of recycling is that it provides a temporal delay (Fox et al. 2009: 101); hence the speaker may want to achieve only one or two beats of delay[2] by recycling function words. High-frequency function words are often phonologically reduced (cf. Jurafsky et al. 1998),[3] which may also contribute to late repair initiation in monosyllabic words (Fox et al. 2009: 100). For early repair initiation in replacing repairs, they also offer a possible explanation. They suggest that in several languages, there is a preference for early initiation in replacing repairs just because speakers generally replace content words (Fox et al. 2009: 101), and content words tend to be longer in most languages in their study. This argumentation is not plausible for the Hungarian findings, because we have seen that in the replacing repairs of the corpus word length plays a more important role than syntactic class (Section 6.2.2). In other words, the speakers of the Hungarian corpus generally replace multisyllabic content words because most multisyllabic words are content words, and not because content words tend to be longer in the Hungarian corpus.

As far as the site of repair initiation and word length in Hungarian are concerned, we have seen that the only word-length category where the speakers of the Hungarian corpus show no preference for site of initiation is the category of bisyllabic words. Let us take a closer look at this word-length category in Hungarian. Examining the site of repair initiation, the type of the repair operation, and the syntactic class of the target word in bisyllabic words, we find an interesting category of repair in this word length, which shows a different pattern from our previous observations: this category is recycling initiated in *content* words, *before* the word is recognisably complete.

6.2.5 Bisyllabic words and restarting repair

As we can see in Table 6.11 and Figure 6.7, there are nearly the same number of bisyllabic words in early and late initiation in the Hungarian corpus. To explain this balance in an indirect way by the functions of the two repair operations would only be possible if there were approximately as many bisyllabic words employed in recycling repairs as in replacing repairs. That is, in that case we could assume that most of the recycling repairs are initiated after, and most of the replacing repairs are initiated before recognisable completion. However, this is not the case, even though the observed frequency of bisyllabic function words and bisyllabic content words is also balanced (56 bisyllabic function words and 51 bisyllabic content words) (Table 6.12, Figure 6.8),[4] and even though most of the bisyllabic content words are repaired before recognisable completion, and most of the bisyllabic function words are repaired after recognisable completion (Table 6.13, Figure 6.9).

Table 6.12: Repair in bisyllabic words (Németh 2012: 2032, Table 14)

	Replacing repairs	Recycling repairs	Total
Bisyllabic content words	23 (45%)	28 (55%)	51
Bisyllabic function words	9 (16%)	47 (84%)	56
Total	32 (30%)	75 (70%)	107

$\chi^2(1) = 10.72^*$, $p < .01$; Cramér's V = .317* (strong association between the two variables), $p < .01$

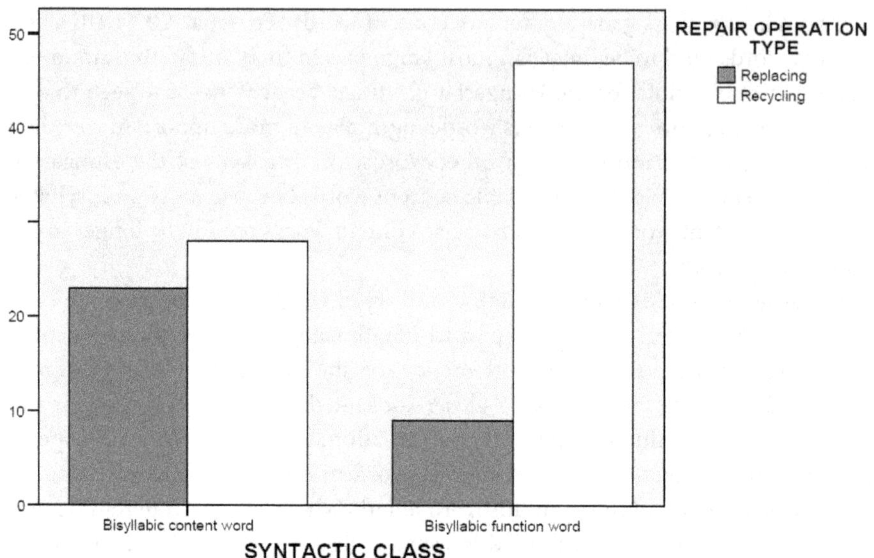

Figure 6.8: Repair in bisyllabic words

Table 6.13: Site of initiation in bisyllabic words (Németh 2012: 2032, Table 13)

	Not recognisably complete	Recognisably complete	Total
Bisyllabic content words	34 (67%)	17 (33%)	51
Bisyllabic function words	15 (27%)	41 (73%)	56
Total	49 (46%)	58 (54%)	107

$\chi^2(1) = 17.10^*$, $p < .01$; Cramér's V = .400* (very strong association between the two variables), $p < .01$

Although the result of the chi-square goodness-of-fit test for the distribution of bisyllabic content words with respect to repair type is not significant ($\chi^2(1) = .49$, $p > .05$), contrary to our expectations, there are more bisyllabic content words involved in recycling repairs than employed in replacing repairs (Table 6.12, Figure 6.8). Early repair initiation is still more frequent in the case of bisyllabic content words than in the case of bisyllabic function words – the result of the chi-square goodness-of-fit test for the distribution of bisyllabic content words with respect to repair initiation is significant ($\chi^2(1) = 5.66^*$, $p < .05$), (Table 6.13, Figure 6.9). These results draw attention to bisyllabic content words which are recycled before recognisable completion, i.e., restarted (Example (54)).

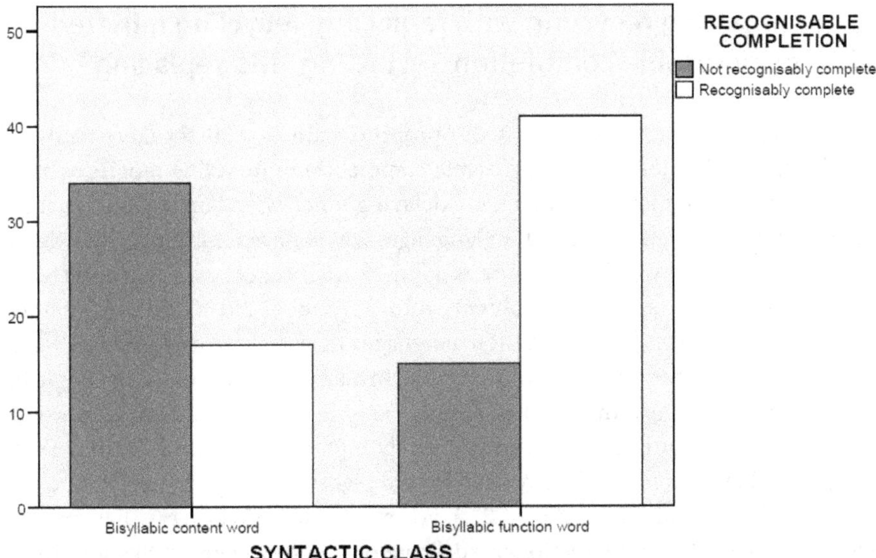

Figure 6.9: Site of initiation in bisyllabic words

(54) (bea004f003: 211)

01 B: *ehhez*   *ha-*   *hadd*   *tegyek*   *hozzá*   *némi*   **gy-**
        this.ALL   le-   let.IMP.2SG.DEF   put.IMP.1SG   PVB   some   gy-

02 **győri**   *emléket*   *is.*
    Győr.ADJDER   memory.ACC   also
    '**Le-** **let** me add some memories to this from **Gy- Győr.**'

I will regard restarting repair as a recycling repair which is initiated before the word is recognisably complete.[5] Restarting in this sense is a type of recycling repair. Although the Hungarian results show the same pattern as the one Fox et al. (2010: 2503) predict, namely, that recycling often affects function words preceding content words and its function in these cases is likely to delay the next content word due, in the Hungarian corpus 74% of the restarted words are content words. In Section 6.3, I attempt to find a possible explanation for this difference between recycling repairs initiated before and after recognisable completion and propose a preference hierarchy among recycling initiated after recognisable completion, restarting, and replacing. In proposing this hierarchy, I will find connections between the results related to replacing, the results related to restarting, and the results related to recycling with late repair initiation in my examinations and in the previous literature.

6.3 Comparing recycling with replacing: recycling initiated after recognisable completion, restarting, and replacing

The universal pattern Fox et al. (2009) propose, namely, that speakers tend towards repair initiation after recognisable completion in recycling repairs, makes them suppose that recycling often has a delaying function in languages (Fox et al. 2009: 80). We have also seen that, in languages which have function words which precede the content words they serve as adjuncts to, speakers tend to recycle back to function words rather than content words (Fox et al 2010: 2504). Fox et al. (2010: 2503) also suggest that in these languages the speakers use function word recycling to delay the next content word due. In all their three languages (English, Hebrew, and German), the speakers tend to recycle back to function words, but replace content words at a disproportionately high rate (Fox et al. 2010: 2487). They note that content words may need to be replaced because they are inapposite (Fox et al. 2010: 2503; see Section 6.2.2). Fox et al. (2009: 85) also say that content words are likely to be interactionally delicate or inappropriate. In Section 6.2.1, I used the same argument when explaining the frequent use of function word recycling as a practice to delay the next content word due. On the basis of this argumentation, I assume that in the languages where speakers tend to use function word recycling to delay the next content word due and replacing to replace content words, *the function of recycling repair and the function of replacing repair may not be independent of each other.* While recycling provides the speaker with extra time so that s/he can select the appropriate item, replacing appears when the articulation of an inappropriate item has already begun, i.e., the selection was not satisfactory. Continuing this train of thought, I suppose that while replacing comes into action when an inappropriate segment has already been produced, recycling may be employed to prevent the speaker from producing inappropriate segments. This hypothesised preventive function, however, is not in conflict with the repair status of recycling. The problem which makes the speaker interrupt the ongoing turn in these cases is the *danger* of producing inappropriate item(s). Going even further, if it is plausible that recycling may be employed to prevent the speaker from producing inappropriate segments, it is also plausible that speakers may employ recycling in order to avoid producing inappropriate segments that would make replacing necessary. That is to say, it is plausible that speakers may employ recycling in order to avoid replacing.

We have seen that the speakers of the Hungarian corpus tend to recycle back to monosyllabic function words (see Section 6.2.1) and to replace multisyllabic content words (see Section 6.2.2). However, while in recycling repair syntactic class plays a more important role than word length, in replacing repairs word length plays a more important role than syntactic class. If we found that most of the function word recyclings in the Hungarian corpus occur before multisyllabic words, the hypothesis that speakers may employ recycling repair to avoid replacing repair could be supported empirically. Table 6.14 displays the result of this examination.[6]

Table 6.14: Word length after function word recycling in the Hungarian corpus (Németh 2012: 2028, Table 7)

Monosyllabic words	Bisyllabic words	Multisyllabic words
65 (35%)	55 (29%)	67 (36%)

In Table 6.14 we can see that the analysis of all the function word recyclings does not conform to our previous expectations. Function word recyclings are distributed evenly with respect to the length of the word following them ($\chi^2(2) = 1.326$, $p > .05$ → not significant). The number of monosyllabic words delayed by function word recycling is nearly the same as the number of multisyllabic words delayed in the same way. To find an explanation for this, we have to differentiate between the recycling of different function words. While the recycling of articles may indicate a word search process and usually occurs before content words, the recycling of conjunctions or relative pronouns may indicate a clause search process in Hungarian and, in this way, can be followed by function words as well. The variability of syntactic class can be eliminated if we test function word recyclings projecting an upcoming noun phrase, for example, article recyclings (Example (55)).

(55) (SZTEPSZI 3: 818)

01 B: *és* *akkor* *ugye* ***a*** ***a*** *részeg* *az* *mondjuk*
and then you.know the the drunk that so.to.say
'and then you know **the the** drunk so to say

02 *elkezd* *kötekedni* *vagy* *verekedni*
PVB.starts provoke.INF or fight.INF
is starting to provoke or fight'

Although the sample is quite small, in Table 6.15 the frequency of article recyclings is directly proportional to the length of the word delayed by this strategy (the result of the chi-square goodness-of-fit test for the distribution of article recyclings with respect to the length of the word following them is significant, i.e., their distribution is not random ($\chi^2(2) = 23.17^*$, $p < .01$). Since the speakers of the Hungarian corpus tend to replace multisyllabic words (see Section 6.2.2), this finding supports the presumption that they may employ recycling to avoid replacing.

Table 6.15: Word length after article recycling in the Hungarian corpus (Németh 2012: 2029, Table 8)

Monosyllabic words	Bisyllabic words	Multisyllabic words
2 (6%)	9 (25%)	25 (69%)

It is interesting to remark that one of the two monosyllabic words delayed by article recycling is a German word in the corpus (it occurs when the speakers are talking about second language acquisition).

Although Fox et al. (2010) do not examine the syntactic class of words following function word recycling in their three languages, their finding that the speakers tend to use function word recycling to delay the next content word due and replacing to replace content words supports the hypothesis. This assumption about the potential preventive function of recycling may serve as an explanation for the difference between the number of recycling and replacing self-repairs in the Hungarian corpus, in the corpora of Fox et al. (2010), and in all the languages which have function words preceding content words and in which replacing repairs are initiated mainly in content words. According to my hypothesis, the speakers in these languages may avoid the necessity of employing replacing in content words by recycling the function words immediately preceding them. However, we can see a difference between the number of recycling and replacing self-repairs not only in the languages with the morpho-syntactic structure mentioned above, but in all the languages examined so far. Let us consider the table displaying the number of self-repair instances in the languages examined by Fox et al. (2009) and Fox et al. (2010), supplemented by the Hungarian results (Table 6.16).

Fox et al. (2009: 101) claim that in the corpora of their seven languages, replacing repairs are generally initiated in content words. On the basis of the examination of English, Hebrew, and German, Fox et al. (2010: 2504) predict that verb-initial and verb-medial languages tend to have function words preceding content words. As far as the structures of the languages examined by Fox et al. (2009) are concerned, their sample is typologically, genetically, and areally diverse: Indonesian is verb-medial and prepositional, Sochiapam Chinantec is verb-initial and prepositional, Japanese is verb-final and postpositional, Mandarin is verb-medial and prepositional, Bikol is verb-initial and prepositional, and finally, Finnish is verb-medial, with both prepositions and postpositions (Fox et al. 2009: 61–62).

Table 6.16: Recycling and replacing repair in the languages examined so far (Németh 2012: 2029, Table 9)

	Recycling repair	Replacing repair	Total
English	111 (76%)	36 (24%)	147
Hebrew	128 (83%)	27 (17%)	155
German	98 (69%)	44 (31%)	142
Indonesian	117 (80%)	29 (20%)	146
Sochiapam Chinantec	185 (92%)	16 (8%)	201
Japanese	147 (73%)	53 (27%)	200
Mandarin	115 (77%)	35 (23%)	150
Bikol	162 (88%)	23 (12%)	185
Finnish	116 (72%)	46 (28%)	162
Hungarian	415 (75%)	142 (25%)	557

The sources are the following. The English, Hebrew, and German data are from Fox et al. 2010; the Indonesian, Sochiapam Chinantec, Japanese, Mandarin, Bikol, and Finnish data are from Fox et al. 2009, and the source of the Hungarian data is Németh 2012.

It is striking that in all the languages examined – and not only in those with function words before content words – there are more recycling repairs than replacing repairs in Fox et al.'s (2009, 2010) corpora. Is it possible that recycling is a universally more preferred repair operation than replacing? If so, what can be the reason for that?

Fox et al. (2009: 80) make a remark which has an interesting implication:

Recycling tends to be initiated after recognisable completion, as it is frequently employed to delay the next content word due. The only exception to this is Japanese, *where recycling repairs are generally initiated prior to recognisable completion* and where function words generally follow content words. (emphasis mine)

This implies the following: in Japanese, function word recycling cannot be used to delay the next content word due, therefore recycling repairs do not tend to be initiated after recognisable completion: restartings are over-represented in the language (see the Japanese example of Fox et al. 1996: 207 as Example (56)).

(56) (Fox et al. 1996: 207)

M: *tteyuuka* *koko* *denwa* **kaket-** **kakete** *kite* *sa,*
    I.mean here telephone ca call come FP (final particle)
    'I mean, (they) **ca- called** us here,'

Considering the length[z] and syntactic class of words in which Japanese speakers initiate recycling, Fox et al. (2009: 85) point out that Japanese is unique among their languages because it has the lowest rate of short words in which speakers initiate recycling repairs (only 5% of the recycled words are monosyllabic in the Japanese corpus). They explain this observation by the low frequency of one-mora words in the language. They note that these one-mora words are mainly postpositions (see Example (56)), and as postpositions generally follow their nouns instead of preceding them, they are usually not used to delay the next content word due (Fox et al. 2009: 86). Furthermore, 68% of the bisyllabic words and 93% of the multisyllabic words recycled are content words in the Japanese corpus (Fox et al. 2009: 91–92). Since recycling repairs are generally initiated prior to recognisable completion in Japanese, we can say that the restarted words tend to be content words in the language. This result is similar to the Hungarian findings: 74% of the restarted words are content words in the Hungarian corpus.

Although Fox et al. (2009) do not explore the syntactic class of the restarted words in their languages, we can acquire some information concerning the length of words in which the speakers of their seven languages employ restarting repair. In order to acquire this information, we have to examine their tables showing the relationship between site of initiation and word length in recycling repair. Their corpora (except for the Japanese corpus) contain so few instances of restarting repair, that it seems reasonable to consider bi- and multisyllabic words together. Since the speakers of the Hungarian corpus also prefer late repair initiation in recycling repair, I follow the same strategy when presenting the Hungarian results relating to word length in restarting repair.

Table 6.17: Site of initiation of simple recycling repair initiated in monosyllabic words (Table 3.9 in Fox et al. 2009: 81)

	Not recognizably complete	Recognizably complete	Total
Sochiapam Chinantec	4 (3%)	137 (97%)	141
Indonesian	1 (4%)	24 (96%)	25
Mandarin	5 (6%)	86 (94%)	91
Bikol	7 (12%)	43 (88%)	50
English	39 (16%)	209 (84%)	248
Finnish	8 (21%)	30 (79%)	38

Table 6.18: Site of initiation in recycling repairs in words of three or more syllables (Table 3.11 in Fox et al. 2009: 84)

	Not recognizably complete	Recognizably complete	Total
Mandarin	1 (33%)	2 (67%)	3
Indonesian	12 (46%)	14 (54%)	26
English	7 (70%)	3 (30%)	10
Finnish	24 (77%)	7 (23%)	31
Japanese	80 (87%)	12 (13%)	92
Bikol	61 (91%)	6 (9%)	67
Sochiapam Chinantec	1 (100%)	0 (0%)	1

From Jack Sidnell (ed.), *Conversation Analysis: Comparative Perspectives* © Cambridge University Press 2009. Reproduced with permission of Cambridge University Press through PLSclear.

Table 6.19: Site of initiation of recycling repairs in bisyllabic words (Table 3.15 in Fox et al. 2009: 89)

	Not recognizably complete	Recognizably complete	Total
Indonesian	17 (26%)	49 (74%)	66
Mandarin	6 (29%)	15 (69%)	21
Finnish	20 (43%)	27 (57%)	47
Bikol	20 (44%)	25 (56%)	45
English	12 (44%)	15 (56%)	27
Sochiapam Chinantec	21 (49%)	22 (51%)	43
Japanese	26 (55%)	21 (45%)	47

From Jack Sidnell (ed.), *Conversation Analysis: Comparative Perspectives* © Cambridge University Press 2009. Reproduced with permission of Cambridge University Press through PLSclear.

Comparing Table 6.17, Table 6.18, and Table 6.19, we realise that all the restarted words are bi- and multisyllabic, and 75% of the restarted words are multisyllabic in the Japanese corpus. As far as the other languages are concerned, 85% of the restarted words are bi- and multisyllabic in Finnish and Sochiapam Chinantec, 97% of the restarting repairs affect bi- and multisyllabic words in Indonesian, and 92% of the restarted words are initiated in bi- and multisyllabic words in Bikol. Mandarin and English do not show such a high frequency of bi- and multisyllabic words in restarting repair: while 58% of the restarted words are bi- and multi-syllabic in Mandarin, only 33% of the English restartings are initiated in longer words. Regarding the Hungarian corpus, 83% of the restarting repairs occurred in bi- and multisyllabic words. Consequently, although the other languages have fewer restarted words in their corpora than Japanese, we can see similar tendencies in these languages as regards the length of words affected by restarting. Thus, restarting tends to affect longer words cross-linguistically.

Let us consider the syntactic class and length of the words in which speakers initiate replacing in the languages studied by Fox et al. (2009). Although the authors do not present their results relating to syntactic class language by language, they claim that replacing repairs are generally of content words in their corpora (Fox et al. 2009: 101). They have not examined the length of words affected by replacing repair in their languages either, but we can find information about this if we compare the figures in Table 6.20, Table 6.21, and Table 6.22. While Table 6.20 displays the site of initiation of replacing repairs initiated in monosyllabic words, Table 6.21 shows the same information regarding words of three or more syllables. Although Fox and her colleagues do not present a similar table for bisyllabic words, the number of the instances of this category involved in replacing repair in the seven languages can be calculated by taking into consideration the two tables mentioned above and the total numbers of replacing repairs in the languages (Table 6.22).

Table 6.20: Site of initiation of simple replacement repair initiated in monosyllabic words (Table 3.10 in Fox et al. 2009: 82)

	Not recognizably complete	Recognizably complete	Total
Indonesian	0 (0%)	0 (0%)	0
Bikol	0 (0%)	3 (100%)	3
Finnish	0 (0%)	4 (100%)	4
Japanese	0 (0%)	5 (100%)	5
Mandarin	2 (6%)	28 (94%)	30
Sochiapam Chinantec	1 (8%)	11 (92%)	12
English	17 (50%)	17 (50%)	34

The word-length categories affected by replacing show a similar picture to the one we have seen in the case of restarting repair: 100% of the replaced words are bi- and multisyllabic in the Indonesian corpus, 87% of the replacing repairs are initiated in bi- and multisyllabic words in Bikol, 91% of the replaced words are bi- and multisyllabic in Finnish, and 91% of the replacing repairs affect bi- and multisyllabic words in the Japanese corpus. There are three languages in their sample whose speakers tend to replace monosyllabic words. In Sochiapam

Table 6.21: Site of initiation in replacement repairs in words of three or more syllables (Table 3.12 in Fox et al. 2009: 84)[1]

	Not recognizably complete	Recognizably complete	Total
Bikol	8 (62%)	5 (38%)	13
Finnish	7 (64%)	4 (36%)	11
Indonesian	10 (83%)	2 (17%)	12
Finnish	27 (87%)	4 (13%)	31
Japanese	31 (89%)	4 (11%)	35
English	4 (100%)	0 (0%)	4
Sochiapam Chinantec	0 (0%)	0 (0%)	0
Mandarin	0 (0%)	1 (100%)	1

[1] In this table of Fox et al. (2009: 84) there are two rows for Finnish with different figures. This does not affect the result of the present calculation, because we need only the total number of replaced bi- and multisyllabic words in Finnish, and for this it is enough to know the number of replaced monosyllabic words and the total number of replacing repairs in Finnish.

From Jack Sidnell (ed.), *Conversation Analysis: Comparative Perspectives* © Cambridge University Press 2009. Reproduced with permission of Cambridge University Press through PLSclear.

Table 6.22: The total numbers of replacing repairs in the languages examined by Fox et al. (2009: 63)

	Replacing repairs
Indonesian	29
Sochiapam Chinantec	16
English	54
Japanese	53
Mandarin	35
Bikol	23
Finnish	46

Chinantec, only 25% of the replacing repairs are initiated in bi- and multisyllabic words, but the Sochiapam Chinantec corpus contains only 16 replacing repairs, which is the smallest replacing corpus in the sample. The other two languages are Mandarin and English: while 14% of the Mandarin replacing repairs are initiated in bi- and multisyllabic words, 37% of the replaced words are bi- and multisyllabic in the English corpus. Interestingly, of the languages investigated, Mandarin and English are the only two in which restarting repair does not tend to affect bi- and multisyllabic words (see above). As far as Hungarian is concerned, 65% of the replacing repairs are initiated in bi- and multisyllabic words in the Hungarian corpus (see Table 6.2b in Section 6.2.1). I have explained this relatively low frequency of longer words in the repair operation, for example, by reference to the frequent article replacing in the corpus (see Section 6.2.2).

All things considered, we can say that restarting (i.e., recycling initiated before recognisable completion) and replacing tend to affect the same word-length and syntactic class categories in the languages examined so far. They tend to be initiated in bi- and multisyllabic words in Japanese, Finnish, Indonesian, Bikol, and Hungarian, and do not tend to be initiated in bi- and multisyllabic words in English and Mandarin. As to syntactic classes, in Japanese and Hungarian (the only languages in which both restarting and replacing have been examined in this respect), the repair operations tend to be initiated in content words.

It seems that restarting may have the same potential delaying function as recycling initiated after recognisable completion, but its position is different. We have seen that recycling often affects monosyllabic words and function words preceding content words (Section 6.2.1). We have also seen that restarting does not support this pattern: it is often initiated in bi- and multisyllabic words and content words (see this section above). I suppose that this difference is due to the different positions of recycling initiated before and recycling initiated after recognisable completion: both types of recycling have a delaying function, i.e., they provide the speaker with extra time, but while recycling with late initiation delays the word that follows (i.e., it treats a problem related to the upcoming word), restarting delays the rest of the word in which it is initiated, i.e., the problematic word seems to be the one that has already begun. In other words, in the case of restarting, the speaker interrupts the ongoing turn to gain extra time only when s/he has already started the articulation of a problematic word. This may be a potential explanation for the different kinds of words affected by the two types of recycling: while function-word recycling initiated after recognisable completion can delay the next content word due, content-word recycling initiated before recognisable completion, i.e., the restarting of a content word, can delay the rest of the word. Why might it be necessary to delay only the rest of a word? It can happen that a word turns out to be potentially problematic for the speaker only when its articulation has already begun, and by recycling the beginning of the word the speaker can gain extra time to deal with that problem and will not produce inappropriate segments. Of course, restarting repairs may also have other functions than the kind of delaying function described here. According to my hypothesis, then, both types of recycling can be employed to prevent the speaker from producing inappropriate segments, and thus both may be employed to help the speaker in avoiding replacing. The only difference is that while recycling initiated after recognisable completion is used before the problematic, potentially inappropriate word, restarting is initiated when this word has already begun. This means that both restarting and replacing tend to be initiated in potentially inappropriate words. This assumption is supported by the finding that restarting and replacing tend to affect the same word-length and syntactic class categories in the languages examined so far.

If my hypothesis is plausible, in languages where function words follow content words, there must be more restarting repairs because the speakers do not have the opportunity to gain extra time by recycling function words (initiated after recognisable completion) before the production of content words (which may potentially be more problematic). That is to say, if speakers cannot recycle back to a function word in order to delay a content word, they will be more likely to restart the problematic word just to avoid replacing. The Japanese results of Fox et al. (2009) support this hypothesis: we have seen that in the Japanese language function words tend to follow content words, and recycling repairs tend to be initiated prior to recognisable completion (Fox et al. 2009: 80). We can explain this by assuming that, if speakers cannot use recycling repair initiated after recognisable completion where they need extra time, they will use a restarting repair in order to avoid producing inappropriate segments and, thus, in order to avoid the necessity of a replacing repair. This also explains why there are approximately as many recycling repairs relative to the number of replacing repairs in these languages as in the languages where function words tend to precede content words. The proportions are nearly the same: although the delaying function of function-word recycling is missing, there are not fewer recycling repairs and more replacing repairs in Japanese (see Table 6.16). Hence, we can suppose that there is a preference hierarchy among recycling initiated after recognisable completion, restarting, and replacing. To establish this preference hierarchy, I rely on Bilmes (1988) and Sacks (1995b). Although Sacks never defined his notion of preference (he only gave examples), Bilmes (1988: 163) reconstructed its main aspects, one of which is the principle of ordering. According to this principle, there are situations where the speakers' possible choices are ordered in the following way: 'Do *X*, unless you have reason not to, in which case, do *Y*, unless you have reason not to, in which case, do *Z*, and so forth' (Bilmes 1988: 163, emphasis original). I apply this principle of ordering to recycling initiated after recognisable completion, recycling initiated before recognisable completion, and replacing in the following way: if recycling initiated after recognisable completion is available to delay a problematic word, speakers will use it. If not, they will be more likely to employ a restarting repair (recycling initiated before recognisable completion) than use the repair operation of replacing. Replacing always remains the last resort among the three.[8] We can also assume that the ratio of early and late initiations in recycling repairs depends on the typical orders of function and content words in languages, i.e., the exploitability of the delaying function of function-word recycling. In other words, while the recycling to replacing ratio is likely to be approximately universally constant, within recycling repairs the ratio of early to late initiations seems to depend on the morpho-syntactic structures of languages. This is in accordance with the previous studies illuminating the strong relationship between grammar and repair (see, e.g., Schegloff 1979; Fox et al. 1996; Rieger 2003; Lerch 2007; Fox et al. 2009; Fox et al. 2010) and points to the interaction between grammar and pragmatics.

To sum up, in this chapter I have compared two repair operations: recycling and replacing. The starting point for my investigation was that Fox and her colleagues' (2009, 2010) collections of self-repair instances contain many more recycling than replacing repairs in all the languages examined in both studies (cf. Fox et al. 2009: 63; Fox et al. 2010: 2490) (Table 6.1). As a next step, I considered whether Hungarian fits the patterns suggested as universal. My frequency analysis in the Hungarian corpus has shown that recycling is a much more frequent repair operation than replacing. Furthermore, I have found that the speakers of the Hungarian corpus recycle back most frequently to monosyllabic function words and tend to replace multisyllabic content words. I have also observed that, while in recycling repair syntactic class plays a more important role than word length, in replacing repairs word length plays a more important role than syntactic class in the Hungarian corpus. The result regarding function-word recycling corroborates Fox et al.'s (2010: 2504) prediction, namely, that languages with function words preceding their respective content words will show a preference for recycling back to function words rather than content words so as to delay the next content word due. With respect to site of initiation, Hungarian also fits the cross-linguistic patterns: while recycling tends to be initiated after recognisable completion, replacing is generally initiated before the word is recognisably complete. As speakers initiate repair mainly in monosyllabic words, they tend towards initiation after recognisable completion, but they show no preference for site of initiation in bisyllabic words. The observed frequencies of bisyllabic words by syntactic class, repair type, and site of initiation in the corpus have drawn attention to bisyllabic content words which are recycled before recognisable completion, i.e., restarted.

This observation led to a cross-linguistic comparison of recycling initiated after recognisable completion, restarting, and replacing. I realised that, while recycling initiated after recognisable completion and replacing tend to affect different categories of word length and syntactic class across languages, we can see similar tendencies as regards the length and syntactic class of words affected by restarting and replacing.

I have assumed a preference hierarchy among recycling initiated after recognisable completion, restarting, and replacing: if speakers cannot use recycling initiated after recognisable completion where they need extra time, they will rather use a restarting repair just to avoid the replacing of the problematic word. This hypothesis offers a possible explanation not only for the possibly universal preference for recycling over replacing, but for the possibly universally constant recycling to replacing ratio, as well.

To sum up the argumentation of Chapter 6 from a metatheoretical point of view, it is clear that the data use and methodology of the research phase introduced above was very complex. First, relying on the statistical analyses of Fox et al. (2009) and Fox et al. (2010), I conducted a similar statistical analysis on recycling and replacement in Hungarian. This statistical analysis relied on the qualitative analysis of a Hungarian corpus and the selection of 415 recycling and 142 replacement self-repair instances from the corpus. Then, taking into consideration data from ten languages, I found connections between the results concerning early and late initiated recycling and replacement in the languages. I found these connections intuitively: I stumbled on various bits of information from various previous studies and my own analysis, then integrated these data by using my intuition. Setting up the preference hierarchy between the three repair types also occurred on the basis of my intuition: I found connections between the type of words involved in restarting and replacing and the functions of these repair types intuitively. Consequently, in this chapter I have integrated the qualitative and statistical analysis of a corpus and my intuition. Without the integration of these two kinds of data source it would have been impossible to set up the preference hierarchy model of the three types of self-repair.

In this section, I have regarded the avoidance of inappropriate segments and the avoidance of the necessity of replacing as similar efforts on the part of the interlocutors. The findings of Chapter 6 pose a new question, which serves as a motivation for Chapter 7. Why do speakers cross-linguistically seem to make efforts to avoid producing inappropriate segments that could make replacing necessary? And why does the use of recycling repair seem to be more preferred than producing inappropriate segments?

When speakers produce inappropriate segments, they obviously override the preference for progressivity: their action cannot progress towards possible completion. However, when speakers employ recycling repair, they also override the preference for progressivity: if they repeat the same word(s), the action cannot progress towards possible completion either. Otherwise, recycling could not be regarded as a repair operation, because, according to the definition of repair (see Schegloff et al. 1977; Kitzinger 2013), a phenomenon can be categorised as repair only if the speaker interrupts the ongoing course of action when applying it. In the next chapter, I will argue that the reason for the over-representation of recycling in the corpora should be sought in the difference between recycling and replacing in the way they violate the preference for progressivity. I will argue that producing inappropriate segments violates the preference for progressivity in more respects than repeating an otherwise appropriate element in a conversation. In Chapter 7, I will argue that it is not only the interactional function of a particular repair operation that matters when we select it to treat a problem in talk-in-interaction, but there is a difference between the ways the various repair operation types violate the preference for progressivity, and this difference can make a repair operation less or more preferred in talk-in-interaction.

In Chapter 7, I develop the preference hierarchy model that I have elaborated between the two types of recycling and replacing into another model which is able to describe any repair operations relative to each other. The basis of this model will be one of the inherent properties of repair, namely, that it overrides the preference for progressivity. First, I recall what the notion of preference and the preference for progressivity means in talk-in-interaction from a conversation analytic perspective, then I explore four repair operation types from the point of view of how they violate the preference for progressivity. In order to see the similarities and differences among them, it is necessary to invent a new conceptual framework in which I can examine exactly what happens in the course of the turn from a technical point of view when a repair operation is used by the speaker. I will isolate three features that can technically prevent the turn from moving forward to the next relevant element.

CHAPTER 7

Hypothesis on the preference hierarchy of repair operations

7.1 The notion of preference in conversation analysis

The notion of preference has always been one of the fundamental concepts of conversation analysis. It has been defined as a social/interactional feature of the interactants' orientations to their talk (Schegloff 2007: 61). Its core idea is that speakers follow (often implicit) principles when they act and react in interactional situations (Pomerantz and Heritage 2013: 210). Instead of analysing the speakers' psychological states and their individual attitudes towards their possible actions and the methods of designing their turns, the term *preference* refers to a ranking of alternatives which is institutionalised (Heritage and Atkinson 1984: 53), in other words, to regularities which speakers observably orient themselves to when taking part in a conversation. We can differentiate between preferences relating to the character of the action a turn implements and preferences affecting the construction of the turn (Schegloff 1988, 2007). The first group involves the attitudes taken towards the success of actions. For instance, it is preferred to accept and dispreferred to refuse an invitation. These kinds of preferences may be in conflict with each other. For example, it is preferred to agree with a compliment, but it is also preferred to avoid self-praise (Pomerantz 1978: 88–89) (see Example (33) in Section 5.2, in which the speaker uses turn-constructional delaying practices when delivering self-praise). The second group of preferences has to do with the design of the turn. If an invitation is designed in the following way: *Don't you want to come to my birthday party?*, it is preferred to accept it regarding the character of the action, but the design of the question anticipates the answer *No.*

Preference principles work in different domains and involve various types of constraints and orders (Pomerantz and Heritage 2013: 210). They appear when speakers select and interpret referring expressions (see Sacks and Schegloff 1979), produce and interpret initiating and responding actions (see Sacks 1995a, b), employ repair practices (see Section 3.2), in the turn-taking system (see Stivers and Robinson 2006), and in the progression of action sequences (Pomerantz and Heritage 2013: 210). Let us see what preference means in this last domain.

7.2 The preference for progressivity

As was noted, preference principles play an important role in the progression of action sequences (Pomerantz and Heritage 2013: 210). According to Schegloff (2007: 14), most types of organisation involve the default relationship between their components such that each component should follow the previous one. He emphasises that moving from one element to a hearably-next-one (i.e., what is hearable as a/the next one due) with nothing intervening is the embodiment of progressivity (Schegloff 2007: 17). The term *progressivity* was first used in this sense by Schegloff (1979). It refers to the observation that each component in the organisation of interaction generally progresses to the next relevant element immediately after the prior element (Kitzinger 2013: 239). If anything intervenes between one element and the next one due – if anything violates their contiguity – it will qualify the progressivity of the talk and will be examined for its importance; in other words, it will influence the understanding of the talk (Schegloff 2007: 15). Examining inserting repair, Schegloff (2008) notes that, when speakers employ this repair operation, the preference for progressivity is violated. He asks: 'What sorts of things … warrant such an override, warrant such a marked usage?' (Schegloff 2008, as cited in Wilkinson and Weatherall 2011: 66). This means that there is a general, basic preference for progressivity in talk-in-interaction. Schegloff (2013: 43) argues that the preference for progressivity concerns the overall structural organisation of talk, the basic dynamic of which is progressional and directional toward a possible completion. Speakers' orientation to what comes next is organised on two levels. On the macro-level the talk is moved forward by reference to the action; in other words, speakers orient themselves towards the action which is hearable as the next one due. The micro-level concerns the construction of the turn, which means that speakers also orient themselves towards the next relevant element of the construction (Schegloff 2013: 42).

The preference for progressivity is both an action- and a design-based preference. From a sequential point of view it manifests itself in the rational ordering of turns. This results in an organisation in which each turn is connected to the turns on either side of it (Sacks et al. 1974: 722). The concept of *nextness* is best realised in the minimal unit for sequence construction, which is the adjacency pair. The adjacency pair is composed of two turns produced by two different speakers.

These turns are relatively ordered, that is to say, they can be differentiated into first and second pair parts (Schegloff 2007: 13). The adjacency pair is pair-type related: not every first pair part can be properly followed by any second pair part (Schegloff 2007: 13). For instance, the type-fitted response to a question is an answer (Stivers 2013: 192). Keeping the components of an adjacency pair together is preferred. When a turn contains more than one question and thus provides for the relevance of more than one answer as the expected subsequent action, speakers tend to begin by responding to the last question to preserve the contiguity for at least one adjacency pair (Sacks 1987 [1973]). The preference for maintaining the progressivity of question–answer sequences influences the organisation of turn-taking as well. In multi-party conversations, if a selected next speaker fails to provide an answer, and a nonselected recipient is in a position to respond, it is preferable for the latter to provide the answer and thus preserve the progressivity of the sequence (Stivers and Robinson 2006). Within the turn, the preference for progressivity appears in the relationship between syllables and sounds: each sound and syllable should be followed by the next relevant sound and syllable (Schegloff 2007: 14), and the turn progresses from sub-unit to sub-unit by reference to sounds, syllables, and words (Schegloff 2013: 42).

The domain of repair is 'the set of practices whereby a co-interactant *interrupts the ongoing course of action* to attend to possible trouble in speaking, hearing or understanding the talk' (Kitzinger 2013: 229, emphasis mine). Kitzinger points out that whereas self-initiated repair in the same turn interrupts the progressivity of the turn, other-initiated repair interrupts the progressivity of the sequence (2013: 231). When speakers halt the progressivity of the current turn or sequence to attend to possible trouble in speaking, hearing, or understanding the talk, they override the preference for progressivity because the maintenance of intersubjectivity (i.e., a world known and held in common among the participants) is more important for them (Schegloff 1992: 1296). That is, in repair, the principle of intersubjectivity comes into conflict with the principle of progressivity (cf. Heritage 2007).

Describing ten repair operations, Schegloff (2013: 43) also emphasises that 'in one way or another, [same-turn repairs] intervene to *interrupt the progressivity of the talk*' (emphasis in the original). When a co-interactant uses a repair operation, the progressivity of the ongoing turn-at-talk and thus the progressivity of the ongoing course of action is being suspended:[1] the turn cannot progress to possible completion from the point of interruption (repair initiation) until the completion of the repair. While repair initiation means a 'possible disjunction with the immediately preceding talk' (Schegloff 2000: 207), the repair is completed 'when the speaker resumes the talk that had been suspended' (Kitzinger 2013: 238). Halting the progressivity of the ongoing course of action is thus an inherent feature of repair, and halting the progressivity of the ongoing turn-at-talk is an inherent feature of same-turn self-repair.

Consequently, although we have assumed that recycling is a cross-linguistically more preferred repair operation than replacing, both of them override the preference for progressivity. The preference hierarchy hypothesis proposed suggests that speakers tend to avoid replacing because they tend to avoid producing inappropriate segments, and producing inappropriate segments is less preferred than employing recycling. I will argue below that recycling and replacing can be differentiated from each other based on how they override the preference for progressivity; in other words, how the turn is being suspended when speakers employ them. After identifying the features of halting the progressivity of the turn in recycling and replacing, I extend this analysis to inserting and aborting so as to see whether these features appear in other repair operations as well.

7.3 Halting the progressivity of the turn by using repair operations

7.3.1 Halting the progressivity of the turn by recycling

In this section I explore precisely what happens when progressivity is being suspended by recycling. Now let us observe what prevents the action from progressing to possible completion when the speaker employs this repair operation. In Example (57), we can see four lines from Example (36), in which Marcsi employs recycling as a turn-constructional delaying strategy when referring to a rapper's health problem.

(57) (SZTEPSZI2: 725)

```
07  M:  én      ennek     tök          örülök              mert
        I       this.DAT  very.much    feel.joy.1SG.INDEF  because
        'I am so happy about this (the rapper's success) because

08      szerintem    ilyen    óriási    (.)    hátrányokkal       indul.
        I.think      such     huge             disadvantages.INS  starts
        I think he starts out with huge disadvantages.

09      tehát     baromi      hendikeppel   hogy   hogy   hogy   olyan
        that.is   enormous    handicap.INS  that   that   that   such
        that is with an enormous handicap that that that he is

10      amilyen
        such
        like that'
```

M: I am so happy about that (the rapper's success) because I think he starts
      out with huge disadvantages. that is with an enormous handicap **that that
      that** he is like that

In the example, repair initiation occurs tacitly, without any explicit indication
(cf. Kitzinger 2013: 239). In the moment of repair initiation, Marcsi returns to
an earlier point of the TCU and produces the same item again. Since in the example the conjunction *hogy* 'that' is recycled twice, these steps are repeated, then
Marcsi resumes the talk that she has suspended. I argue that recycling suspends
the progressivity of the current turn in two ways. On the one hand, returning to
an earlier point of the TCU means that from a technical point of view the repair
operation is retrospective. The word *technical* is of great importance here, because
in terms of its delaying function recycling is prospective; it operates on upcoming
talk when, for example, it is used in a word search (cf. Fox et al. 2009: 74). On
the other hand, producing the same item for the second or third time (when it
does not express stress or emphasis) means that, although the speaker articulates
something which moves the turn forward phonetically, this part of speech has the
same role in the progression of the action as the first occurrence of the item at
issue. The progression of the action is similar to when a record needle gets stuck
and just plays the same tune over and over again. In this sense, but only in this
sense, i.e., from the point of view of progressivity, the second or third occurrence
of the same item is redundant. However, since it facilitates attending to possible
problems in speaking, hearing, or understanding the talk, producing the same
item for the second or third time as a repair operation is necessary in accomplishing the action. One could ask why it is necessary to differentiate between
retrospectivity and redundancy when isolating them as the features contributing
to halting progressivity in the case of recycling. Their roles in the phenomenon
might be understood better if we consider cases in which redundant elements by
themselves prevent the action from progressing, without involving any retrospective steps. For example, when the speaker uses fillers or hesitation markers, s/he
does not go back, but the action still 'gets stuck' (see Example (28) repeated below
as Example (58)).

(58) (bea004f003: 200)

01 E: *arra*   *gondoltunk*   *Mártá(.)val*   *hogy*   **ö:**
         that.SUB   thought.1PL.INDEF   Márta.COM   that   **u:h**
         'Márta and I have been thinking about **u:h**

02   *szeretnénk*   *önt*   *megkérdezni*   *hogy*   *a*   <u>*ka*</u>*rácsonyt*
         like.COND.1PL.DEF   you.ACC   PVB.ask.INF   that   the   Christmas.ACC
         asking you how (.)

03	*azt*	*(.)*	*hogyan*	*töltötte*		*ön?*	*meg*	*hogyan*
	that.ACC		how	spent.3SG.DEF		you	and	how

you spent Christmas? and how

04	*szokott*	**ma-**	**önöknél**	*zajlani?*	*(.)*	*az*	*egész*
	used	yo-	you.PL.ADE	happen.INF		the	whole

is it celebrated at **yo- your** place? (.) the whole

05	*(.)*	*ünnep?*
		holiday

(.) Christmas holiday?

(1.0)

06	T:	*na*	*jó.*
		now	good

alright.

(2.0)

07	T:	*akkor*	*kezdjék*	*maguk!*
		then	begin.IMP.3PL.DEF	you.PL

but you should begin!'

E: Márta and I have been thinking about **u:h** asking you how (.) you spent
Christmas? and how is it celebrated at **yo- your** place? (.) the whole (.)
Christmas holiday?
(1.0)
T: alright.
(2.0)
T: but you should begin!

In line 01, Enikő stretches ö, which is a non-lexical filler in Hungarian. Both this
stretching and the sequential environment of the phenomenon suggest that it
serves as a turn-constructional delaying strategy in the example. Let us recall that
Enikő, a student, uses the filler before she addresses Tibor, an older man, for the
first time. Analysing the example in Section 5.1, I have assumed that a formal
and hierarchical social relationship is established between the participants in this
example, which is supported by the replacing occurring later, i.e., the less formal
form of address *maguknál* 'at your place' is replaced by the more formal *önöknél*
'at your place' in line 04. Since ö: ('u:h') occurs just before Tibor is addressed
for the first time (at the end of line 01), it is likely to be the first sign of Enikő's
insecurity in addressing the man. In Section 5.2, I have argued that if recycling or
practices such as *uh(m)*, *y'know*, and silence (and *ö* in Hungarian) are employed
solely to delay the next item due so that the speaker can attend to possible trouble

in speaking, hearing, or understanding the talk, then we should interpret them as repair. Since it alters the turn in some interactionally consequential way, the production of *ö:* in the example should be analysed as repair. Let us see how it prevents the action from progressing to possible completion. This time the speaker does not go back but articulates a new element. Although this new element carries the turn forward phonetically, as in the case of recycling, it does not contribute to the progression of the action. In this sense, but again only in this sense, we can say that, although they are necessary for carrying out the action, elements like *ö* are redundant from the point of view of progressivity.

7.3.2　Halting the progressivity of the turn by replacing

Now let us explore how replacing overrides the preference for progressivity. In line 04 of Example (58), Enikő starts the articulation of *maguknál* but cuts it off and replaces it with another form of address, *önöknél.* How is the turn being suspended in this case? What are the similarities and/or differences relative to recycling?

In the moment of repair initiation, the speaker also returns to an earlier point of the TCU (the repair is initiated with a cut-off in the example); therefore, like recycling, from a technical point of view, replacing is retrospective. Since in terms of its function, replacing changes the preceding talk, we can say that it is retrospective both from a technical and a functional point of view. However, in this case Enikő does not produce the same item again but substitutes the part of speech between her repair initiation and the earlier point she has returned to with a new item. Similarly to producing the same item again, producing one item instead of another is also redundant from the point of view of progressivity: the new item plays the same role in the TCU as the replaced segment; the action gets stuck.[2] Nonetheless, unlike a record needle which plays the same tune over and over, this time the action is 'on the wrong track'. That is, it is not enough that it does not progress to possible completion; it has gone in an inappropriate direction. I will refer to this third feature of halting progressivity as inappropriateness.

Consequently, while recycling is assumed to override the preference for progressivity in two respects (retrospectivity and redundancy), replacing prevents the turn from progressing to possible completion in three respects: retrospectivity, redundancy, and inappropriateness. As halting the progressivity of the ongoing turn is an inherent property of each repair operation, it seems to be an ideal basis on which any two repair operations can be described relative to each other. This assumption makes it well motivated to extend the research to further repair operations. Below I add inserting and aborting to the operations examined.

7.3.3 Halting the progressivity of the turn by inserting

Let us consider the inserting in Example (47), repeated here as Example (59).

(59) (SZTEPSZI2: 790)

```
01  Á:  a      média    nem    föltétlenül    (.)    a    (.)    csak    a
        the    media    not    necessarily           the        only    the
        'the media is not necessarily (.) guided by (.) only by
```

```
02      jóindulat    v:ezérli.      hogy    majd    tehetséget    faragunk
        goodwill     guides.DEF     that    then    talent.ACC    carve.1PL.INDEF
        goodwill. the intention of making a talent
```

```
03      belő[le
        of.her/him
        of somebo[dy
```

Á: the media is not necessarily (.) guided **by (.) only by** goodwill. the intention
    of making a talent of somebo[dy

In the example, Ági begins to give her opinion about what the leading ethical principle of the Hungarian media can be. After the definite article she goes back and inserts *csak* 'only' into the TCU, which creates a concessive form: goodwill can be one of the leading principles of the Hungarian media. Of the three repair operations examined so far, the feature of retrospectivity appears most obviously in the case of inserting. Even Wilkinson and Weatherall's description of the repair operation includes this retrospective step: 'speakers halt their talk-in-progress to go back and add something else into the turn before resuming' (2011: 65). Thus, inserting changes the TCU by adding extra elements into it afterwards. Since the speaker goes back but does not change the part of speech between the repair initiation and the earlier point she has returned to, resuming the talk that has been suspended makes it necessary to have a repeated part in the TCU. Therefore, like recycling, inserting bears the features of redundancy and retrospectivity when overriding the preference for progressivity. The only difference between the techniques of the two repair operations is that inserting adds extra elements to the TCU. The progressivity of the turn, however, would not be suspended only by adding extra elements to it; the reason for halting progressivity is that these extra elements are added afterwards, making it necessary to have a repeated part in the TCU.

7.3.4 Halting the progressivity of the turn by aborting

In aborting, the speaker casts off the ongoing TCU and starts the same action in a different way, in a different form, with a different TCU (cf. Laakso and Sorjonen 2010: 1153). In Example (60), which is five lines from Example (49), Linda invokes her acquaintances' opinion on the effects of marijuana.

(60) (SZTEPSZI8: 1067)

01 L: *hát*   *nekem*   *akik*   *ö*   *ismerőseim*
        well   to.me   who.PL   uh   acquaintances.POSS.1SG
        'well my acquaintances who

02   *mondták*   *ők*   *nem*   *nem*   *ezt*   *mondták*
        told.3PL.DEF   they   not   not   this.ACC   said.3PL.DEF
        have told me this it's not it's not what they said

03   *hanem*   *inkább*   *azt*   *hogy-*   *vagy*   *több*   (.)
        but   rather   that.ACC   that   or   several
        but rather- or I have heard several (.)

04   *olyat*   *hallottam*   *hogy*   *mondjuk*   *szar*   *volt*
        such.ACC   heard.1SG.INDEF   that   so.to.say   shit   was.3SG
        opinions that so to say it felt like shit

05   *vagy*   *vagy*   *rossz*   *volt*   [*utána*]
        or   or   bad   was.3SG   after.it
        or or it felt bad [after it]

L: **well my acquaintances who have told me this it's not it's not what they said
    but rather- or I have heard several (.) opinions that so to say it felt like shit
    or or it felt bad [after it]**

At first, Linda refers to all of her acquaintances who have told her their experiences with using marijuana (*ők* 'they' in line 02), but in line 03 she initiates an aborting repair with a cut-off and restricts the category of referents to 'several opinions': *vagy több (.) olyat hallottam* ('or I have heard several (.) opinions'). In the moment of repair initiation, Linda returns to the beginning of the TCU (retrospectivity) and substitutes the part of speech between the repair initiation and the earlier point she has returned to, i.e. the whole TCU-so-far with a new TCU which is intended to implement the same action as the one substituted. As far as the progressivity of the action is concerned, producing a new TCU instead of another one is redundant: the new TCU implements the same action as the replaced TCU was to implement. Consequently, until the speaker resumes the talk that has been suspended because of the repair, the progression of the activity gets stuck. Again, it is important to emphasise that *redundant* does not mean *unnecessary*. Moreover, as in the case of replacing, it is not enough that the action does not progress to possible completion; it has gone in an inappropriate direction. Since aborting can be regarded as replacing a TCU with another TCU, from a technical point of view it does not differ from replacing: it suspends the progressivity of the turn in three respects: retrospectivity, redundancy, and inappropriateness.

7.4 The preference hierarchy model of repair operations

Table 7.1 displays the respects in which recycling, replacing, inserting, and aborting halt the progressivity of the turn. Although the four repair operations are diverse regarding their possible functions, I have assumed that recycling and inserting, and replacing and aborting override the preference for progressivity in the same respects. While recycling and inserting violate the preference for progressivity in the respects of redundancy and retrospectivity (two respects), replacing and aborting contain redundant *and* inappropriate elements besides the retrospective step in their techniques, and therefore override the preference for progressivity in the respects of redundancy, retrospectivity, and inappropriateness.

Table 7.1: The respects in which recycling, replacing, inserting, and aborting suspend the progressivity of the turn

	Recycling	Inserting	Replacing	Aborting
Redundancy	+	+	+	+
Retrospectivity	+	+	+	+
Inappropriateness	−	−	+	+

The starting point for my argumentation in the present section has been the assumption that speakers tend to avoid replacing because they tend to avoid the production of inappropriate segments, and producing inappropriate segments is less preferred than employing recycling. The exploration of recycling and replacing in terms of the way they override the preference for progressivity seems to offer a theoretical basis for this assumption. Producing inappropriate segments and replacing them with new items suspends the progressivity of the turn, i.e., it overrides the preference for progressivity in more respects than employing recycling does. I suppose that the more respects a repair operation overrides the preference for progressivity, the less preferred it will be in talk-in-interaction. This would offer a possible explanation for the cross-linguistic difference assumed between the frequency of recycling and the frequency of replacing. However, we know that the various repair operations may have various functions; in other words, they can contribute to the maintenance or restoration of intersubjectivity in various ways.

We have seen that the maintenance of intersubjectivity is built into the procedural organisation of interaction (Schegloff 1992: 1299) because the maintenance of the ongoing activity is possible only if there is a world which the interactants know and hold in common (Schegloff 1992: 1296) (see Section 3.2 above). We have also seen that there is a preference for maintaining the progressivity of the ongoing activity in talk-in-interaction (Sacks 1987 [1973]; Stivers and Robinson 2006; Schegloff 2007, 2013; Kitzinger 2013). In repair, the principle of progressivity comes into conflict with the principle of intersubjectivity (cf. Heritage 2007). In order to restore intersubjectivity, speakers have to override the preference for progressivity when they use the procedural infrastructure of the repair mechanism (Schegloff 1992). These statements suggest that there is a one-way relationship between the principle of intersubjectivity and the principle of progressivity, namely, intersubjectivity has an impact on progressivity when the necessity of its restoration makes speakers override the preference for progressivity. However, my hypothesis, stating that the more respects a repair operation overrides the preference for progressivity, the less preferred it will be in talk-in-interaction, suggests that it is possible for speakers to make an effort to violate progressivity in the fewest possible respects. That is, although different repair operations aim to solve different problems in interaction, the act of selecting among them is also sensitive to how they override the preference for progressivity. This is possible only if we propose a two-way relationship between intersubjectivity and progressivity: the principle of progressivity also has its impact on the principle of intersubjectivity. I assume that during turn-design, speakers tend to make an effort to violate the preference for progressivity in the fewest possible respects, which will influence their maintenance of intersubjectivity. This is only possible if they tend to make an effort to avoid problems which potentially require repair, or if they cannot do so, they will tend to avoid problems which potentially require repair operations overriding the preference for progressivity in several respects. In speakers' choices of repair operations, then, I assume the interaction of the principle of intersubjectivity manifesting itself in the functions of repair operations and the principle of progressivity manifesting itself in the way they suspend the progressivity of the turn.

To sum up, I assume a preference hierarchy among repair operations. Relying on Sacks's (1995b) principle of ordering reconstructed by Bilmes (1988: 163), I claim that if X, Y, and Z are repair operations, and X overrides the preference for progressivity in one, Y in two, and Z in three respects, then speakers will not interrupt the progressivity of the ongoing turn unless they have reason to do so, in which case, they will employ X unless they have reason not to, in which case, they will employ Y unless they have reason not to, in which case, they will employ Z. For example, since employing replacing or aborting prevents the turn from progressing to possible completion in three respects, under my hypothesis these two repair operations are less preferred than recycling and inserting, which suspend progressivity only in two respects.

Now, let us see how this hypothesis affects the speakers' selections among repair operations in actions where they use more than one repair operation one after the other.

7.5 Applying the preference hierarchy hypothesis to actions where speakers use more than one repair operation

7.5.1 The relationship between repair operations implemented in the same action

Earlier studies suggest that there is no one-to-one relationship between the repair operation type and the particular interactional task it fulfils (Wilkinson and Weatherall 2011; Németh 2017). For example, both replacing and inserting can upgrade the force of the action in English (see Example (24) and Example (38) again):

(24) (Kitzinger 2013: 243)

Clt: If there's anybody that you fee:l .hhh i̲s̲n't supporting you then: **you can ch- you have- you have the a̲b̲solute right to ch̲a̲nge** that person

(38) (Wilkinson and Weatherall 2011: 81)

Pre: I'm n̲o̲w at thee **ne̲:w (0.2) spa̲n̲king ne̲w** (.) We̲dgwood museum in Stoke on Tre:nt. hh A:: (.) ve̲ry swi̲sh ne:w modern buil:ding

Moreover, different repair operations may not only have the same kind of interactional function, but it is also possible that more than one repair operation fulfils one and the same interactional task in the same turn and in the same action, addressing in this way the same problem (cf. Schegloff 1979: 278).

In Example (61), Ági tells Zsuzsi and Marcsi that once she met and talked to the star of a Hungarian reality show in a pub, who revealed that the events of his reality show are prearranged by the TV station. The man in question belongs to the Roma minority, which is recognisable in the show through his manner of speaking.

(61) (SZTEPSZI2: 803)

01 Á: *és   akkor   elkezdett   velünk   beszélgetni,   és   akkor*
    and   then   started   with.us   talk.INF   and   then
    'and then he started talking to us, and then

02 *elmondta   hogy   °jaj   nehogy   azt*
    PVB.said.3SG.DEF   that   oh   not   that.ACC
    he told us that °oh, you shouldn't

03 *higgyétek   má.   meg   van   tervezve   az   egész.*
    believe.IMP.2PL.DEF   already PVB   is   planned   the   whole
    believe it at all. the whole show is prearranged.

04 *fel   fogok   borulni   februárban   autóval   izé.°*
    PVB   will.1SG.INDEF   overturn.INF   February.INE   car.INS   and.so.on
    my car will overturn in February, and so on.°

05 **de   hogy   ilyen   egész   norm-   tehát   hogy   ö   (.)   nem: hm:**
    but   that   such   quite   norm-   that.is that   uh   not   u:mm
    but like quite norm- that is, uh (.) he didn't u:mm

06 **nem: hasz-   nem   volt   akcentusa:**
    not   use-   not   was.3SG   accent.POSS.3SG
    didn't use- didn't have an accent'

Á: and then he started talking to us, and then he told us that °oh, you shouldn't
    believe it at all. the whole show is prearranged. my car will overturn in
    February, and so on.° **but like quite norm- that is, uh (.) he didn't u:mm**
    didn't use- didn't have an accent

When Ági reveals the cheating of the reality show to her co-participants, she lowers her voice (her quieter talk is between degree signs in lines 02–04). This suggests that she is sharing secret, inside information. In line 05, she breaks off – *de hogy ilyen egész norm-* ('but like quite norm-') – and starts anew with the reformulation marker *tehát* ('that is'), which supports the analysis of this phenomenon as aborting repair. Ági immediately starts another TCU which underlies the same action: *tehát hogy ö (.) nem: hm: nem: hasz- nem volt akcentusa:* ('that is, uh (.) he didn't u:mm didn't use- didn't have an accent'). The new TCU, which contains several hesitancy markers and the recycling *nem: hm: nem:* ('didn't u:mm didn't'), is closed by a replacing: Ági breaks off again and replaces *nem: hasz-* ('didn't use-') with *nem volt akcentusa* ('didn't have an accent'). Why is it so difficult for Ági to design this TCU?

In order to find an answer to this question, it is useful to examine the action that the TCU implements. Ági tells the others that the famous man in the pub did not speak in the way he usually does in the show; in other words, his manner of speaking (e.g., his pronunciation) did not show that he is a Roma. Drew, Walker, and Ogden say that 'self-repair affords us the most direct access to the alternative versions or selections considered by speakers, whatever was initially selected being rejected by the speaker in favour of the subsequent version, the repair' (2013: 92). In the present example, we can see the alternative versions Ági selects in order to refer to the man's manner of speaking. As she has to distinguish between a Roma and a non-Roma manner of speaking, she is being very cautious to avoid discrimination. It is very likely that the first cut-off is in the word *normális* ('normal'),[3] which is an adjective that would be quite offensive: calling non-Romas' manner of speaking 'normal' would imply that Romas' manner of speaking is not normal. Perhaps that is why Ági is loath to say it and tries to find another solution. She selects the negative form *nem: hm: nem: hasz-* ('didn't u:mm didn't use-'), which she finally replaces with yet another negative form: *nem volt akcentusa:* ('didn't have an accent'). The new form contains the impersonal substantive verb *volt* ('was') instead of the action verb *használ* ('use'), which makes the description of the man's manner of speaking more impersonal and further decreases the chance of offending him. Therefore, in this example, the repair operations aborting, recycling, and replacing are used for the same purpose: to avoid offensive language when referring to a Roma man's non-Roma manner of speaking.

In the above example, the speaker changes her turn several times to bring it closer to a turn-version which she orients to as (more) appropriate for its sequential environment, for the action it is designed to perform, and for the recipient to whom it is addressed (Drew et al. 2013). As was mentioned above, these changes become visible through self-repairs: self-repair affords us access to the work of turn-design, to speakers' orientations as to how they should construct the turn in the best way. Self-repair in this way shows us the alternative versions of the turn, the version which is initially selected and then rejected, and the subsequent version in favour of which the previous one is rejected (Drew et al. 2013: 92) (Figure 7.1).

The forms the rejected and selected turn-version take always depend on the particular case and the particular function of the repair operation in question. The turn-version which the speaker orients to as more appropriate is always the

self-repair

INITIALLY SELECTED TURN-VERSION   →   SUBSEQUENT TURN-VERSION

less appropriate   more appropriate

Figure 7.1: Changing the turn by self-repair

one which helps in accomplishing the speaker's aims, which manifest themselves in the functions of self-repair. In the case of an inserting repair with a specifying function, for example, the rejected turn-version is the version without the inserted segment, while the version which the speaker considers more appropriate is the one which contains the specifying term as well (e.g., not only *cemetery*, but *Cary cemetery* in Wilkinson and Weatherall's example 2011: 73). In the case of a recycling with a delaying function, the turn-version which is more appropriate is the one which is able to gain extra time for the speaker, i.e., the one which contains each occurrence of the repeated segment. However, if the recycling is used at the emergence of overlapping talk in order to deal with possible problems in hearing or understanding caused by simultaneous talk (Schegloff 2013: 59–60; cf. Schegloff 1987), the speaker repeats some stretch of talk in order to say it in the clear (Schegloff 2013: 60). Consequently, in this case, the rejected turn-version seems to be the one containing only the overlapped occurrence(s) of the repeated item, while the turn-version considered more appropriate by the speaker seems to be the one containing only the occurrence(s) produced in the clear.[4]

Let us see how the repair operations in Example (61) show how the speaker's orientation always moves towards increasingly appropriate turn-versions.

(61) (SZTEPSZI2: 803)

05	*de*	*hogy*	*ilyen*	*egész*	*norm-*	*tehát*	*hogy*	*ö*	*(.)*	*nem:*	*hm:*
	but	that	such	quite	norm-	that.is	that	uh		not	u:mm

but like quite norm- that is, uh (.) he didn't u:mm

06	*nem:*	*hasz-*	*nem*	*volt*	*akcentusa:*
	not	use-	not	was.3SG	accent.POSS.3SG

didn't use- didn't have an accent'

The first turn-version Ági selects in order to refer to the showman's manner of speaking is cut off in line 05 (*de hogy ilyen egész norm-* 'but like quite norm-'). As I claimed in the analysis of this example before, it is quite plausible that Ági is trying to find another expression instead of *normal* when referring to the non-Roma manner of speaking; therefore, she is aborting the turn-so-far and selecting a negative construction (*tehát hogy ö (.) nem:* 'that is, uh (.) he didn't'), which she considers more appropriate. In other words, she rejects the turn-so-far and starts the same action again. Then, she repeats the negative form (*nem: hm: nem:* 'didn't u:mm didn't'). Let us assume that this recycling has a delaying function: it provides Ági with extra time to select a less offensive alternative. In this case, the rejected turn-version is the one containing only the first occurrence of the negative form (*tehát hogy ö (.) nem:* 'that is, uh (.) he didn't'), and the version which she considers more appropriate is the one with the repeated negative, i.e., which provides her with extra time: *tehát hogy ö (.) nem: hm: nem: hasz-* 'that is, uh (.) he didn't u:mm didn't use-'). Then even this turn-version is cut off: Ági replaces *nem: hasz-* 'didn't use-' with *nem volt akcentusa:* 'didn't have an accent'. Hence the recently selected turn-version becomes a rejected turn-version again, and the finally selected turn-version, which is the result of a replacing repair, is as follows: *tehát hogy ö (.) nem: hm: nem volt akcentusa:* 'that is, uh (.) he didn't u:mm didn't have an accent'. Figure 7.2 shows the relationship between the turn-versions generated by the repair operations aborting, recycling, and replacing carried out one after the other in the same action, when the speaker is describing a Roma man's non-Roma manner of speaking in Example (61).

Employing several repair operations one after the other in the same turn and in the same action thus means that the turn-version which is selected by the first operation will be the same version as the one which is rejected by the second one; and the turn-version which is selected by the second operation will be the version rejected by the third operation, and so on (Figure 7.3).

Figure 7.3 shows that, if the speaker employs more than one repair operation one after the other in the same turn while accomplishing the same action, then the repair operations following one another cannot be independent of each other. They are interconnected by the turn-versions they generate: the turn-version

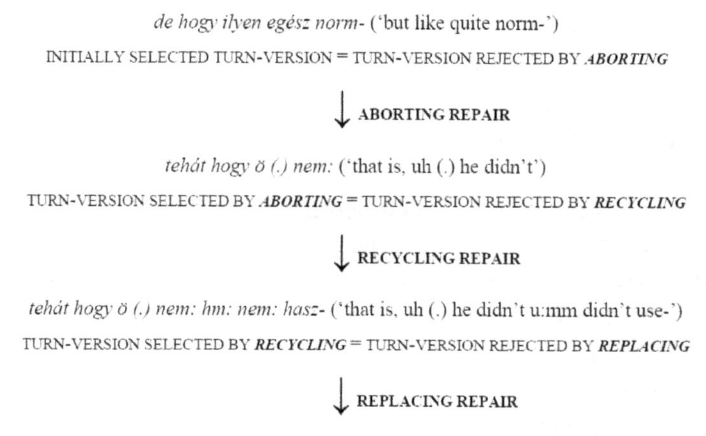

Figure 7.2: Changing the turn by self-repairs carried out one after the other in the same action in Example (61)

SPEAKER'S ORIENTATION

LESS APPROPRIATE

INITIALLY SELECTED TURN-VERSION =

= TURN-VERSION REJECTED BY SELF-REPAIR (1)

↓ SELF-REPAIR (1)

TURN-VERSION SELECTED BY SELF-REPAIR (1) =

= TURN-VERSION REJECTED BY SELF-REPAIR (2)

↓ SELF-REPAIR (2)

TURN-VERSION SELECTED BY SELF-REPAIR (2) =

= TURN-VERSION REJECTED BY SELF-REPAIR (3)

↓ SELF-REPAIR (3)

TURN-VERSION SELECTED BY SELF-REPAIR (3)

MORE APPROPRIATE

Figure 7.3: Changing the turn by several self-repairs carried out one after the other in the same action

selected by the first operation will be the one rejected by the second operation, the turn-version selected by the second operation will be the one rejected by the third operation, and so on, until the speaker designs the final turn-version. Since every repair operation changes the turn in some way, every successive one changes the turn-version which has been changed by the previous one. Therefore, every repair operation has an effect on the next possible operation. In other words, a speaker's selection among repair operations at a certain point of the turn must have an effect on the next possible selection; what is more, in an indirect way it has an effect on every further selection among repair operations following it.

Furthermore, I argue that if every self-repair changes the turn in some way to make it (more) appropriate for its sequential environment, for the action it is designed to perform, and for the recipient to whom it is addressed (Drew et al. 2013), then each of them will generate a rejected and a selected turn-version. Consequently, if there is more than one self-repair employed one after the other in the same action, it does not matter whether they address the same problem or not: the rejected and selected turn-versions will be intertwined in the same way as we could see in Example (61). Even if they have different functions, if more than one self-repair is employed in the same turn and in the same action, the repair operations that follow one another cannot be independent of each other: every selection among them will affect the next possible selection, and in an indirect way every further selection as well.

Let us see an example, where, although more than one self-repair is performed by the speaker while accomplishing the same action, these repair operations address different problems. Example (13) in Section 3.1 showed how turns are fashioned out of turn-constructional units and how these turn-constructional units embody actions. Now let us consider this extract as Example (62) from another point of view. Cili and Anna talk about Christmas. Anna is raising the question of when a couple should decide to celebrate Christmas together.

(62) (bea003n001)

```
01  C:  bővül     a       család    még       jobban.
        grows     the     family    even      more
        'the family becomes even bigger.

        (0.3)

02  A:  hát     igen.   de      ez      is      olyan   nehéz      hogy      igazából
        well    yes     but     this    also    so      difficult  that      actually
        well, yes. but it is also so difficult that

03      amikor    már        valaki:        hosszabb    ideje    együtt
        when      already    somebody       longer      time     together
        when actually you: have been going out with somebody for a longer time

04      van     valakivel            hogy    hogy    mikor    jön       az
        is      somebody.COM         that    that    when     comes     that
        that that when does

05      a      el     az     a      pont     amikor    már        együtt
        the    PVB    that   the    point    when      already    together
        the time come to

06      is      karácsonyoznak
        also    celebrate.Christmas.3PL.INDEF
        also celebrate Christmas together'

C:  the family becomes even bigger.
    (0.3)
A:  well yes. but it is also so difficult that when actually you: have been going out
    with somebody for a longer time that that when does the time come to also
    celebrate Christmas together
```

The first action in the example is a *telling* in line 01 by Cili (cf. Schegloff 2007: 7). The second action is Anna's response in line 02, which constitutes the first TCU of her turn. The second unit in Anna's turn implements a problem-raising. She is wondering when the time comes for a couple to also celebrate Christmas together. The TCU implementing this action contains two self-repairs which orient to different problems. First, in line 04, Anna recycles the conjunction *hogy* 'that'. This is a function word occurring at the beginning of clauses in Hungarian (cf. Lerch 2007: 127). As the recycling of conjunctions and relative pronouns may indicate a clause search process in Hungarian (see Section 6.3), it is well motivated to analyse this phenomenon as the repair operation of recycling (see Section 5.2). Applying the analysing method just proposed, we can say that the version initially selected by Anna is as follows: *de ez is olyan nehéz hogy igazából amikor már valaki: hosszabb ideje együtt van valakivel hogy* 'but it is also so difficult that when actually you: have been going out with somebody for a longer time that'. Then the turn is changed by a recycling; the turn-version selected by the recycling is: *de ez is olyan nehéz hogy igazából amikor már valaki: hosszabb ideje együtt van valakivel hogy hogy mikor jön az a* 'but it is also so difficult that when actually you: have been going out with somebody for a longer time that that when does the'. Then, the turn-version selected by the recycling will be rejected by another repair operation, namely, an inserting repair by Anna. With the conjunction *hogy* 'that' she starts a subordinate clause: *hogy mikor jön az a* (*hogy* 'that' *mikor* 'when' *jön* 'comes' *az* 'that (demonstrative determiner)' *a* 'the'). After the demonstrative determiner *az* 'that' and the definite article *a* 'the', which introduce a noun phrase in Hungarian, she interrupts the progressivity of the turn, goes back in the TCU, and inserts the preverb *el* immediately after the verb *jön*. The preverb, which is usually written together with the verb as a prefix + verb unit, is a subtype of verb modifiers in Hungarian (É. Kiss 2002: 57). The difference between *jön* 'come' and *eljön* 'come' is that *eljön* carries an additional meaning: its agent is expected to come. In this example, it emphasises that the time when a couple decides to celebrate Christmas together does not come unexpectedly but is an ordinary event in a developing relationship. Since wh-interrogative phrases have an inherent [+focus] feature (É. Kiss 2002: 90), in the clause Anna starts, *mikor* 'when' should be in the focus position immediately before the verb *jön*. In these cases, the prefix should come immediately after the verb which it modifies. However, since Anna has already pronounced the demonstrative determiner *az* 'that' and the definite article *a* 'the' after the verb, she has to go back and insert the prefix *el* before *az a* (*mikor jön az a el az a pont* 'when does the time come').[5] The newly selected (and final) turn-version is therefore as follows: *de ez is olyan nehéz hogy igazából amikor már valaki: hosszabb ideje együtt van valakivel hogy hogy mikor jön el az a pont amikor már együtt is karácsonyoznak* 'but it is also so difficult that when actually you: have been going out with somebody for a longer time that that when does the time come to also celebrate Christmas together' (Figure 7.4).

> *de ez is olyan nehéz hogy igazából amikor már valaki: hosszabb ideje együtt van valakivel*
> *hogy* ('but it is also so difficult that when actually you: have been going out with somebody
> for a longer time that')
>
> INITIALLY SELECTED TURN-VERSION = TURN-VERSION REJECTED BY *RECYCLING*
>
> ↓ RECYCLING REPAIR
>
> *de ez is olyan nehéz hogy igazából amikor már valaki: hosszabb ideje együtt van valakivel*
> *hogy hogy mikor jön az a* ('but it is also so difficult that when actually you: have been going
> out with somebody for a longer time that that when does the')
>
> TURN-VERSION SELECTED BY *RECYCLING* = TURN-VERSION REJECTED BY *INSERTING*
>
> ↓ INSERTING REPAIR
>
> *de ez is olyan nehéz hogy igazából amikor már valaki: hosszabb ideje együtt van valakivel*
> *hogy hogy mikor jön el az a pont amikor már együtt is karácsonyoznak* ('but it is also so
> difficult that when actually you: have been going out with somebody for a longer time that
> that when does the time come to also celebrate Christmas together')
>
> TURN-VERSION SELECTED BY *INSERTING* = FINAL TURN-VERSION

Figure 7.4: Changing the turn by self-repairs in Example (62)

To sum up, in this section I have assumed a relationship between the repair operations which are implemented in the same action: I have argued that, even if they have different functions, every selection among them will affect the next possible selection, and in an indirect way every further selection as well. Now let us see how this observation affects our preference hierarchy hypothesis proposed in the previous section.

7.5.2 Selecting among repair operations in actions where speakers use more than one repair operation

The preference hierarchy hypothesis of repair operations says that the more respects a repair operation overrides the preference for progressivity, the less preferred it will be in talk-in-interaction. This implies that it is possible for speakers to make an effort to violate progressivity in the fewest possible respects. The hypothesis thus assumes that, although different repair operations aim to solve different problems in the interaction, the act of selecting among them is also sensitive to how they override the preference for progressivity. This means that I have proposed the interaction of the principle of intersubjectivity manifesting itself in the functions of repair operations and the principle of progressivity manifesting itself in the way repair suspends the progressivity of the turn. I have argued that, when they design their turns, speakers may make an effort to violate the preference for progressivity in the fewest possible respects, and to avoid problems which potentially require repair or less preferred repair operations. The selection among repair operations, then, is influenced not only by the principle of intersubjectivity, but also by the principle of progressivity: it is not only the function of repair operations that matters, but also the way they override the preference for progressivity.

In the previous section it has been shown that when changing the turn in some way, every repair operation generates a rejected and a selected turn-version. If more than one self-repair is performed one after the other in the same turn and in the same action, these turn-versions are intertwined. For this reason, the repair operations following one another in the same turn and action cannot be independent of each other: every selection among them will affect the next possible selection, and in an indirect way every further selection as well. Consequently, the principle of intersubjectivity and the principle of progressivity must affect the selection among repair operations not only locally but also through the intertwining turn-versions: their effect will spread on to the next possible selection, and, in an indirect way, to every further selection (Figure 7.5).

Considering this observation together with the preference hierarchy hypothesis, it seems that the speakers' efforts to violate the preference for progressivity in the fewest possible respects during a selection at a certain point of the turn must have an effect on the next possible selection and, what is more, in an indirect way on every further selection among repair operations. Since every selected repair operation changes the turn in some way so as to make it more appropriate, every further repair operation must therefore deal with a more appropriate turn-version than the previous one. From this it follows that the preference hierarchy hypothesis must have a consequence not only on the selection among repair operations locally, but on every further selection in a linear way during

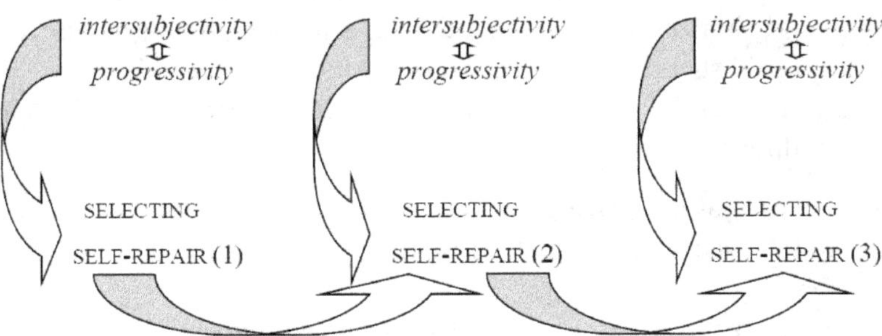

Figure 7.5: Selecting among same-turn repair operations when carrying out the same action

turn-design. If speakers tend to select repair operations overriding the preference for progressivity in the fewest possible respects, and this selection will result in a more appropriate turn-version, then the next possible repair operation must tend to override the preference for progressivity in fewer respects than the previous one. I hypothesise the following tendencies in actions where more than one repair operation is employed one after the other:

[1] Any repair operation will tend to be followed by an operation which violates the preference for progressivity in fewer respects.

[2] If [1] is not fulfilled, then any repair operation will tend to be followed by an operation which violates the preference for progressivity in no more respects than the previous one.

[3] If [2] is not fulfilled, then out of two repair operations violating the preference for progressivity in a different number of aspects, the one following any repair operation tends to be the one that violates the preference for progressivity in fewer respects.

Let us see what this means in the case of our four repair operations under investigation (for the sake of convenience, Table 7.1 is shown again below).

Table 7.1: The respects in which recycling, replacing, inserting, and aborting suspend the progressivity of the turn

	Recycling	Inserting	Replacing	Aborting
Redundancy	+	+	+	+
Retrospectivity	+	+	+	+
Inappropriateness	−	−	+	+

I have argued above that, while recycling and inserting violate the preference for progressivity in the respects of redundancy and retrospectivity (two respects), replacing and aborting contain redundant *and* inappropriate elements besides the retrospective step in their techniques, and therefore override the preference for progressivity in the respects of redundancy, retrospectivity, and inappropriateness (in three respects).

[1] means that a replacing or an aborting, for example, is more likely to be followed by a recycling or an inserting than by another replacing or aborting.

[2] means that if [1] is not fulfilled, a recycling or an inserting, for example, is more likely to be followed by another recycling or inserting than by a replacing or an aborting.[6]

Since we have only four repair operations involved in the present examination, at this stage of the research it is not yet possible to test the preference hierarchy hypothesis. We do not know how the other six repair operation types described by Schegloff (2013) override the preference for progressivity; what is more, there may be other repair operations which have not yet been identified and described in the conversation analytic literature (Schegloff 2013: 68). Therefore, in order to see the tendencies in speakers' selections among repair operations in actions where only one operation is performed, and in those where more than one operation is employed one after the other, further research is needed.

To sum up, in this chapter I have proposed a preference hierarchy model that is able to describe any repair operations relative to each other. The basis of this model is one of the inherent properties of repair, namely, that it overrides the preference for progressivity. After examining recycling, replacing, aborting, and inserting from this point of view, I have identified three aspects in which they can violate the preference for progressivity: redundancy, retrospectivity, and inappropriateness. I have claimed that the more respects a repair operation overrides the preference for progressivity, the less preferred it will be in talk-in-interaction. In speakers' selections among repair operations, then, I suppose the interaction of the principle of intersubjectivity and the principle of progressivity: it is not only the function of a repair operation that matters, but also the way it halts the progressivity of the turn.

Since every repair operation changes the turn in some way to be more appropriate and generates a rejected and a newly selected turn-version, the preference hierarchy hypothesis must have a consequence not only on the selection among repair operations locally, but also on the actions where more than one self-repair is performed one after the other. Since every successive repair operation must deal with a more appropriate turn-version than the previous one, I hypothesise that any repair operation will tend to be followed by an operation which violates the preference for progressivity in fewer respects.

In order to find an answer to the research question as to why repeating the same element seems to be more preferred in a conversation than producing an inappropriate item, in this chapter I have examined same-turn repair operations from a novel perspective. I have isolated three features that characterise the way repair operations suspend the progressivity of the ongoing turn. Without exploring this new aspect of the way same-turn self-repair works in conversation, it would have been impossible to find a candidate answer to my research question. Introducing this new perspective into my investigation has contributed to our knowledge of the phenomenon of self-repair in conversation, enriched the results obtained by earlier examinations from different perspectives, and, at the same time, shown the prismatic nature of the argumentation process in linguistic theorising (see Section 2.3.1; cf. Kertész and Rákosi 2012, 2014).

CHAPTER 8

Conclusion and future directions

My first research questions, introduced at the beginning of this book, are as follows: Is there a cross-linguistic difference between the frequency of recycling and replacing? If so, how can we account for it? Is it possible to analyse and interpret same-turn repair operations relative to each other?

Considering the results related to Bikol, English, Finnish, German, Hebrew, Hungarian, Indonesian, Japanese, Mandarin, and Sochiapam Chinantec, we can assume that yes, there is a cross-linguistic difference between the frequency of recycling and the frequency of replacing. I have proposed a preference hierarchy among recycling initiated after recognisable completion, recycling initiated before recognisable completion (restarting), and replacing: if speakers cannot use recycling initiated after recognisable completion where they need extra time, they will prefer to use restarting just to avoid replacing. This hypothesis offers a possible explanation not only for the possibly universal preference for recycling over replacing, but for the possibly universally constant recycling to replacing ratio, as well. On the basis of the results of Fox et al. (2009), Fox et al. (2010), and the examination of Hungarian, I have proposed that the ratio of early and late initiations in recycling depends on the typical orders of function and content words in languages, i.e., the exploitability of the delaying function of function word recycling. This is in accordance with the previous studies which have described how methods of repair are shaped by the linguistic resources of languages, and argued in this way for the relationship between grammar and repair (see, e.g., Fox et al. 1996; Rieger 2003; Lerch 2007; Fox et al. 2009; Fox et al. 2010) and thus between grammar and pragmatics.

At this stage of the research, I still had to deal with the question of why speakers tend to avoid replacing cross-linguistically.

To answer this question, I added inserting and aborting to the repair operations under investigation and examined the four operations in a larger corpus (see

Chapter 4). In other words, in order to move forward with my argumentation, I found it necessary to extend the context of the research, and so I started a new argumentation cycle, during which I examined repair operations from a different perspective (Kertész and Rákosi 2012: 134–153; 2014: 32–34; Section 2.3.1). I isolated three aspects in which a repair operation can violate the preference for progressivity: retrospectivity, redundancy, and inappropriateness.

As a result of this new argumentation cycle, I developed the preference hierarchy model that I had elaborated between the two types of recycling and replacing into another preference hierarchy model. Since this new model is able to analyse and interpret same-turn repair operations relative to each other, it serves as a potential answer to the main question of this book. It reinterprets the relationship between the principle of intersubjectivity and the principle of progressivity in talk-in-interaction. Saying that the principle of maintaining progressivity also has an impact on the principle of maintaining intersubjectivity (not only the other way around), it assumes a two-way relationship between intersubjectivity and progressivity.

All in all, my findings suggest that during turn-design, speakers' selections among repair operations depend on at least three factors:

- the function of repair operations,
- the number of respects in which they override the preference for progressivity, and
- the morpho-syntactic structure of the language used.

This supports the previous findings highlighting the interaction between grammar and pragmatics.

During the elaboration of the preference hierarchy hypothesis, I have relied on various data sources (see Section 2.2). As direct sources, I used an almost five-hour-long Hungarian spoken corpus consisting of 17 everyday conversations, the results of earlier investigations into ten languages, and the theoretical framework of conversation analysis. I have used my intuition as well, during the following steps:

1. At one of the earliest stages, when identifying linguistic phenomena as instances of the four repair operations in the Hungarian corpus;
2. when assuming connections between the operation of recycling and replacing;
3. when revealing the connections between the data related to replacing and restarting in previous studies;
4. when proposing a preference hierarchy among recycling initiated after recognisable completion, recycling initiated before recognisable completion, and replacing; and

5. when proposing a preference hierarchy among repair operations and considering its consequences on actions where more than one self-repair is performed one after the other.

Furthermore, I have used the statements obtained from the sources listed above as premises of inferences. The conclusion of such an inference receives its plausibility value indirectly, from its premises; consequently, the inferences I made have been indirect sources in my investigation (Kertész and Rákosi 2012, 2014; see Section 2.2).

My argumentation has required the integration of the sources listed above. Kertész and Rákosi (2012: 239) emphasise that relying on as many data sources as possible allows us to assign a higher plausibility value to a hypothesis than would be the case when relying on any of these data sources individually. Since I have relied on several data sources, I assign a high plausibility value to my statements.

My examination has shown that retaining the traditional concepts and methods of conversation analysis but supplying its conceptual and methodological apparatus with new concepts and methods does not undermine the results and principles of this theoretical framework. On the contrary, adding quantitative and statistical methods to the qualitative examination of same-turn self-repair and introducing the concepts of redundancy, retrospectivity, and inappropriateness as the features describing the way same-turn self-repair suspends the progressivity of the ongoing turn introduce a new perspective into the research into same-turn self-repair and extend our knowledge of this interactional phenomenon.

The preference hierarchy hypothesis imposes new questions. Since the features of redundancy, retrospectivity, and inappropriateness do not belong to the four repair operations per se, but to the property of halting the progressivity of the turn, we should add not only the other six repair operations to the research (deleting, searching, parenthesising, sequence-jumping, reformatting, and reordering) (see Schegloff 2013), but all those phenomena which suspend the progressivity of the ongoing course of action in talk-in-interaction. In this way, it would be possible to recognise new repair operations which have not yet been described in the literature (cf. Schegloff 2013: 68) and also phenomena where the progressivity of the course of action is suspended without repair occurring. Taking into consideration all these phenomena, the model could be testable.

Notes

Chapter 1

1. See, for example, Boomer and Laver 1968; Fromkin 1973; Nooteboom 1980, 2005; Levelt 1983, 1989; Cutler 1988; Postma, Kolk, and Povel 1990; Blackmer and Mitton 1991; Kolk and Postma 1997; Clark and Wasow 1998; Poulisse 1999; Postma 2000; Shriberg 2001; Pérez et al. 2007; Gósy 2003, 2004, 2005, 2008, 2012; Markó 2004, 2006; Huszár 2005; Bóna 2006; Horváth 2004, 2007; Fabulya 2007; Gyarmathy 2006, 2007, 2009, 2012a, b; Gyarmathy and Gósy 2014.

2. The empirical observations of the book rely on a nearly five-hour-long corpus consisting of everyday Hungarian conversations from which I take some examples in the introductory part. The corpus is described in detail in Chapter 4. The relevant repair operation is indicated by boldface. Since the punctuation in the extracts does not indicate syntactic but intonational boundaries, I do not use capital letters at the syntactic sentence boundaries. The glosses are not intended to capture all morphological properties of Hungarian words but indicate only the ones necessary for the purposes of the present analysis. For this reason, the glosses include only the grammatical information that is marked by a non-empty morpheme in Hungarian. Where possible I give the corresponding English word in an inflected form. Furthermore, the words in the extracts are not segmented into components by hyphens for two reasons. First, for the purposes of the present research the internal structure of words is not relevant, and second, and more importantly, hyphens are used to indicate cut-off in conversation analysis. The glosses in the examples other than Hungarian are left in their original form as they appear in their sources. The abbreviations used in the glosses can be found in the Abbreviations section. For the sake of convenience, I repeat the English translation of the longer examples at the end of the extracts.

3. The term *trouble-source* thus refers to the particular segment of talk judged problematic by the speaker who initiates repair and should be distinguished from the basis of the problem (e.g., noise).
4. See, e.g., Schegloff, Jefferson, and Sacks 1977; C. Goodwin 1980, 1981; M. H. Goodwin 1983; Heritage 1984; Jefferson 1972, 1974, 1987; Fox, Hayashi, and Jasperson 1996; Drew 1997; Stivers 2005; Robinson 2006; Wilkinson and Weatherall 2011; Schegloff 1979, 1987, 1992, 1997a, b, 2000, 2008, 2013.
5. Since the difference between inserting and parenthesising is merely in the type of the incorporated component, in this book I will analyse the cases of parenthesising as inserting.
6. These factors are the site of repair initiation and the length and syntactic class of words in which repair is initiated.
7. As the trouble-source may consist of more than one word and may be different from the word in which repair initiation occurs, I use the term *target word* when referring to the word in which speakers initiate repair.

Chapter 2

1. True statements and demonstrative inferences are rare in linguistic theorising. However, Kertész and Rákosi (2012: 81) note that if a hypothetically assumed linguistic universal is tested, and the result of the testing is negative, it is often interpreted as a demonstrative inference. They bring Moravcsik's (1969) universal-candidate as an example, which is as follows: (U) If the indefinite article is derived from the cardinal 'one', then non-numerable nouns cannot take an indefinite article. Kertész and Rákosi (2012: 81) argue that this universal can be refuted with the help of the following inference. It is true with certainty that if U, then if the indefinite article was derived from the cardinal 'one' in Coptic, then non-numerable nouns cannot take an indefinite article in Coptic. It is also true with certainty that in Coptic, the indefinite article was derived from the cardinal 'one', but non-numerable nouns can take an indefinite article. From this it follows that the negation of U is also true with certainty.

Chapter 3

1. The term was first used in this sense by Sacks et al. 1974.
2. This point is in accordance with Searle's indirect speech act theory (Searle 1975). In Searle's framework, questioning is the secondary act, requesting the primary illocutionary act (Searle 1975: 62).

3. *Hát* is a discourse marker in Hungarian. Here it may indicate turn-taking and also strengthen Anna's agreeing with Cili (see Dér 2012: 8). On the functions of *hát*, see Schirm 2011.
4. The word that is cut off here is likely to be *vissza* 'back'.

Chapter 4

1. This corpus has been recorded by Ágnes Lerch and the author of the present study. We are grateful to the Institute for Psychology, University of Szeged for making it possible for us to record these nine conversations.
2. I am also grateful to Mária Gósy for putting eight conversations from the BEA-database at my disposal.
3. Since the research can be divided into two phases, in each of which I used the corpus in a different way, I introduce further details of the corpus when describing these two phases of the study.
4. For more on Pearson's chi-square statistics and Cramér's V measure of nominal association, see Section 6.2.1.
5. By multisyllabic words I mean words of three or more syllables.

Chapter 5

1. In some cases, this difference is found in the prosody rather than in the lexicon (Schegloff 2013: 61).
2. *Tök,* meaning 'pumpkin' in Hungarian, in evaluative APs is an upgrading modifier.
3. Here the discourse marker *hát* may indicate that the speaker is about to add some extra information to the turn.
4. Recognisable completion allows the listener to assume that the word is finished (Fox et al. 2009, see Chapter 4).
5. Here and everywhere else in the book, by the expression *inappropriate* word, segment, or item I will mean that the speaker labels the word, segment, or item as inappropriate.
6. The source of Jefferson's TRIO Materials (1967) are a series of three interrelated telephone calls (Jefferson 1974: 199).
7. In Hungary, at oral exams there are usually topics from which the teacher selects one or two for the student to work out.
8. Here and everywhere else the expression *decrease the power of a critical assessment / remark / opinion* means that the speaker softens or mitigates criticism.

9.   Here and everywhere else in the book I use the term *avoid* to refer to the speakers' institutionalised attitudes towards dispreferred actions (cf., e.g., the *error avoidance format* described by Jefferson 1974: 194).
10. In Hungarian, a practice of this kind is *ö:*.
11. Since this novel analysing method needs further, conscious elaboration, it has not yet been applied in the analyses of the present book.
12. On the phenomenon of *rush-through*, see Clayman 2013: 159.
13. *Gáz* 'gas' does not only mean 'aerial material' in Hungarian, but is also a slang adjective. It can be used for describing practically anything negative: it may mean 'bad', 'awkward', 'intolerable', 'unbearable', etc. (e.g., *gáz helyzet* 'bad situation').
14. However, when we analyse the particular occurrences of recycling in conversations, sometimes it can be difficult to identify this function. In these cases, the analysis of other features of the phenomenon (e.g., site of initiation) can help us to decide whether we are dealing with a repair operation or not (see Chapter 6).
15. *Á:* or *á* intensifies negation in Hungarian.
16. In Hungary, women can spend two years at home with their babies, during which time they receive a maternity benefit.
17. The discourse marker *hát* may express emphasis here.
18. These factors are the site of repair initiation, and the length and syntactic class of words in which repair is initiated.
19. As the trouble-source may consist of more than one word, and may be different from the word in which repair initiation happens, I use the term *target word* when referring to the word in which speakers initiate repair.

Chapter 6

1.   The author wishes to thank one of the anonymous reviewers of Németh 2012 for this idea.
2.   One syllable gives roughly one conversational beat of delay (Fox et al. 2009: 96).
3.   We have seen that in the Hungarian corpus most of the function words are monosyllabic (see Table 6.3 in Section 6.2.1).
4.   As the speakers of the Hungarian corpus tend to recycle back to function words and replace content words, this could mean that there are as many bisyllabic words employed in recycling repairs as in replacing repairs.
5.   The term *restart* can also be found in Gósy's (2004) taxonomy, which was elaborated to deal with speech disfluencies from a psycholinguistic point of

view. However, Gósy does not regard restart as a subcategory of recycling. She uses the term for all cases when a word which is not completely pronounced is followed by the same word completely pronounced (see also, Gyarmathy 2009, 2012a).

6. Table 6.14 does not contain function word recyclings followed by other function word recyclings.

7. Instead of syllables, Japanese words are divided into units called mora determining syllable weight. Syllable weight determines stress and timing (Fox et al. 2009: 61). As in the case of the other languages, the study by Fox et al. (2009) refers to the Japanese words as mono-, bi-, and multisyllabic.

8. On the notion of preference, see Section 7.1.

Chapter 7

1. Here the word *being* refers to the observation that suspending the talk by employing a repair operation is not limited to the moment when the turn is interrupted, i.e., to repair initiation.

2. Here again, *redundant* does not mean *unnecessary*.

3. The only other Hungarian words starting with *norm-* and not being the derivations of *norma* ('norm') are *normann* ('Norman') and *Normandia* ('Normandy'). Neither of these fit into the sequential environment of the example.

4. The author would like to thank the audience of her presentation at the 15th IPrA Conference in Belfast, 2017 for the notion that it is not enough to know the repair operation type for the identification of the rejected and selected turn-versions. Their identification is possible only by taking into consideration the particular function of self-repair in each case.

5. This case shows that the location of insertion repair in the TCU depends on the morpho-syntactic structure of the language used. The exploration of this interesting issue in Hungarian requires further studies.

6. Since we now have only two categories of repair operations (recycling/insertion and replacing/aborting), we cannot produce any examples of [3]. However, in Section 7.3.1, a possible analysis of the fillers such as *ö:* in Hungarian has been proposed. This analysis regards these phenomena as repair operations violating the preference for progressivity in only one respect, namely, the respect of *redundancy* (see Extract (58)). This classification requires further refinement.

References

Austin, John L. (1962) *How to Do Things with Words*. Cambridge, MA: Harvard University Press.

Austin, John L. (1979) *Philosophical Papers*. Oxford and New York: Oxford University Press.

Babbie, Earl (2010) *The Practice of Social Research*. Wadsworth: Cengage Learning.

Bilmes, Jack (1988) The concept of preference in conversation analysis. *Language in Society* 17(2): 161–181. https://doi.org/10.1017/S0047404500012744

Blackmer, Elizabeth R., and Mitton, Janet L. (1991) Theories of monitoring and the timing of repairs in spontaneous speech. *Cognition* 39(3): 173–194. https://doi.org/10.1016/0010-0277(91)90052-6

Bolden, Galina B., Mandelbaum, Jenny, and Wilkinson, Sue (2012) Pursuing a response by repairing an indexical reference. *Research on Language and Social Interaction* 45(2): 137–155. https://doi.org/10.1080/08351813.2012.673380

Bóna, Judit (2006) A megakadásjelenségek akusztikai és percepciós sajátosságai [The acoustic and perceptional characteristics of disfluency phenomena]. In Mária Gósy (ed.) *Beszédkutatás 2006* [Speech Research 2006] 101–114. Budapest: MTA Nyelvtudományi Intézet.

Boomer, Donald S., and Laver, John D. M. (1968) Slips of the tongue. *International Journal of Language & Communication Disorders* 3(1): 2–12. https://doi.org/10.3109/13682826809011435

Clark, Herbert H., and Wasow, Thomas (1998) Repeating words in spontaneous speech. *Cognitive Psychology* 37(3): 201–242. https://doi.org/10.1006/cogp.1998.0693

Clayman, Steven E. (2013) Turn-constructional units and the transition relevance place. In Jack Sidnell and Tanya Stivers (eds.) *The Handbook of Conversation Analysis* 150–166. Oxford: Wiley-Blackwell. https://doi.org/10.1002/9781118325001.ch8

Cramér, Harald (1999) [1946]. *Mathematical Methods of Statistics*. Princeton, NJ: Princeton University Press.

Cutler, Anne (1988) The perfect speech error. In Larry M. Hyman and Charles N. Li (eds.) *Language, Speech and Mind: Studies in Honor of Victoria A. Fromkin* 209–223. London: Croom Helm.

Dér, Csilla I. (2012) Beszélőváltások során használt diskurzusjelölők a magyar spontán beszédben [Discourse markers in turn-taking in Hungarian spontaneous speech]. In

Mária Gósy (ed.) *Beszédkutatás 2012* [Speech Research 2012] 132–143. Budapest: MTA Nyelvtudományi Intézet.

Domonkosi, Ágnes (2002) *Megszólítások és beszédpartnerre utaló elemek nyelvhasználatunkban* [Forms of address and elements referring to the partner in conversation]. Debrecen: A Debreceni Egyetem Magyar Nyelvtudományi Intézetének Kiadványai [Proceedings of the Department of Hungarian Linguistics of the University of Debrecen], 79.

Drew, Paul (1997) 'Open' class repair initiators in response to sequential sources of troubles in conversation. *Journal of Pragmatics* 28(1): 69–101. https://doi.org/10.1016/S0378-2166(97)89759-7

Drew, Paul (2013) Turn design. In Jack Sidnell and Tanya Stivers (eds.) *The Handbook of Conversation Analysis* 131–149. Oxford: Wiley-Blackwell. https://doi.org/10.1002/9781118325001.ch7

Drew, Paul, Walker, Traci, and Ogden, Richard (2013) Self-repair and action construction. In Makoto Hayashi, Geoffrey Raymond, and Jack Sidnell (eds.) *Conversational Repair and Human Understanding* 71–94. Cambridge: Cambridge University Press. https://doi.org/10.1017/CBO9780511757464.003

Egbert, Maria M. (1996) Context sensitivity in conversation: Eye gaze and the German repair initiator *bitte*. *Language in Society* 25(4): 587–612. https://doi.org/10.1017/S0047404500020820

Egbert, Maria M. (2004) Other-initiated repair and membership categorization: Some conversational events that trigger linguistic and regional membership categorization. *Journal of Pragmatics* 36(8): 1467–1498. https://doi.org/10.1016/j.pragma.2003.11.007

Egbert, Maria M., Golato, Andrea, and Robinson, Jeffrey D. (2009) Repairing reference. In Jack Sidnell (ed.) *Conversation Analysis: Comparative Perspectives* 104–132. Cambridge: Cambridge University Press. https://doi.org/10.1017/CBO9780511635670.005

É. Kiss, Katalin (2002) *The Syntax of Hungarian*. Cambridge: Cambridge University Press. https://doi.org/10.1017/CBO9780511755088

Fabulya, Márta (2007) Izé, hogyhívják, hogymondjam. Javítást kezdeményező lexikális kitöltőelemek [Lexical fillers initiating self-repair sequences in Hungarian]. *Magyar Nyelvőr* [Hungarian Purist] 131(3): 324–342.

Fox, Barbara A., Hayashi, Makoto, and Jasperson, Robert (1996) Resources and repair: A cross-linguistic study of syntax and repair. In Elinor Ochs, Emanuel A. Schegloff, and Sandra A. Thompson (eds.) *Interaction and Grammar* 185–237. Cambridge: Cambridge University Press. https://doi.org/10.1017/CBO9780511620874.004

Fox, Barbara A., Maschler, Yael, and Uhmann, Susanne (2010) A cross-linguistic study of self-repair: Evidence from English, German, and Hebrew. *Journal of Pragmatics* 42(9): 2487–2505. https://doi.org/10.1016/j.pragma.2010.02.006

Fox, Barbara A., Wouk, Fay, Hayashi, Makoto, Fincke, Steven, Tao, Liang, Sorjonen, Marja-Leena, Laakso, Minna, and Hernandez, Wilfrido Flores (2009) A cross-linguistic investigation of the site of initiation in same-turn self-repair. In Jack Sidnell (ed.) *Conversation Analysis: Comparative Perspectives* 60–103. Cambridge: Cambridge University Press. https://doi.org/10.1017/CBO9780511635670.004

Fromkin, Victoria A. (ed.) (1973) *Speech Errors as Linguistic Evidence*. The Hague and Paris: Mouton.

Goodwin, Charles (1980) Restarts, pauses, and the achievement of a state of mutual gaze at turn-beginning. *Sociological Inquiry* 50(3–4): 272–302. https://doi.org/10.1111/j.1475-682X.1980.tb00023.x

Goodwin, Charles (1981) *Conversational Organization: Interaction between Speakers and Hearers*. New York: Academic Press.

Goodwin, Marjorie Harness (1983) Aggravated correction and disagreement in children's conversations. *Journal of Pragmatics* 7(6): 657–677. https://doi.org/10.1016/0378-2166(83)90089-9

Gósy, Mária (2003) A spontán beszédben előforduló megakadásjelenségek gyakorisága és összefüggései [Co-occurrence and frequency of disfluencies in Hungarian spontaneous speech]. *Magyar Nyelvőr* [Hungarian Purist] 127(3): 257–277.

Gósy, Mária (2004) A spontán magyar beszéd megakadásainak hallás alapú gyűjteménye [An audition-based collection of Hungarian spontaneous speech disfluencies]. In Mária Gósy (ed.) *Beszédkutatás 2004* [Speech Research 2004] 6–18. Budapest: MTA Nyelvtudományi Intézet.

Gósy, Mária (2005) *Pszicholingvisztika* [Psycholinguistics]. Budapest: Osiris Kiadó.

Gósy, Mária (2008) Magyar spontánbeszéd-adatbázis – BEA [A Hungarian spontaneous speech database – BEA]. In Mária Gósy (ed.) *Beszédkutatás 2008* [Speech Research 2008] 194–208. Budapest: MTA Nyelvtudományi Intézet.

Gósy, Mária (2012) Multifunkcionális beszélt nyelvi adatbázis – BEA [A multifunctional spontaneous speech database – BEA]. In Gábor Prószéky and Tamás Váradi (eds.) *Általános Nyelvészeti Tanulmányok XXIV. Nyelvtechnológiai Kutatások* [Studies in General Linguistics XXIV. Language Technology Research] 329–349. Budapest: Akadémiai Kiadó.

Guimaraes, Estefania (2007) *Talking about Violence: Women Reporting Abuse in Brazil*. Unpublished PhD dissertation, University of York, UK.

Gyarmathy, Dorottya (2006) A beszédpercepciós és beszédprodukciós folyamat összefüggései a megakadásjelenségek tükrében [The correlations of speech perception and speech production in the light of disfluency phenomena]. In Pál Heltai (ed.) *MANYE XVI. Tanulmánykötet* [Volume of Studies] *3/2*. 449–455. Gödöllő: Szent István Egyetemi Kiadó.

Gyarmathy, Dorottya (2007) Az alkohol hatása a spontán beszédprodukcióra [The effect of alcohol on spontaneous speech production]. In Mária Gósy (ed.) *Beszédkutatás 2007* [Speech Research 2007] 108–121. Budapest: MTA Nyelvtudományi Intézet.

Gyarmathy, Dorottya (2009) A beszélő bizonytalanságának jelzései: Ismétlések és újraindítások [The cues of speakers' uncertainty: Repetitions and restarts]. In Mária Gósy (ed.) *Beszédkutatás 2009* [Speech Research 2009] 196–216. Budapest: MTA Nyelvtudományi Intézet.

Gyarmathy, Dorottya (2012a) Kétarcú újraindítás [Double-faced restart]. In Alexandra Markó (ed.) *Beszédtudomány* [Speech Science] 50–67. Budapest: ELTE Bölcsészettudományi Kar, MTA Nyelvtudományi Intézet.

Gyarmathy, Dorottya (2012b) Strategies of disfluency repairs in spontaneous speech. *The Phonetician 2011–I/II* 103/104: 88–96.

Gyarmathy, Dorottya, and Gósy, Mária (2014) The characteristics of sublexical errors in spontaneous speech. In Susanne Fuchs, Martine Grice, Anne Hermes, Leonardo Lancia, and Doris Mücke (eds.) *Proceedings of the 10th International Seminar on Speech Production* 166–169. Cologne: University of Cologne.

Have, Paul ten (1990) Methodological issues in conversation analysis. *Bulletin de Méthodologie Sociologique* 27(1): 23–51. https://doi.org/10.1177/075910639002700102

Hayashi, Makoto (2003) Language and the body as resources for collaborative action: A study of word searches in Japanese conversation. *Research on Language and Social Interaction* 36(2): 109–141. https://doi.org/10.1207/S15327973RLSI3602_2

Heritage, John (1984) *Garfinkel and Ethnomethodology.* Cambridge: Polity Press.

Heritage, John (2007) Intersubjectivity and progressivity in person (and place) reference. In Nicholas J. Enfield and Tanya Stivers (eds.) *Person Reference in Interaction: Linguistic, Cultural, and Social Perspectives* 255–280. Cambridge: Cambridge University Press.

Heritage, John, and Atkinson, J. Maxwell (1984) Preference organization. In J. Maxwell Atkinson and John Heritage (eds.) *Structures of Social Action: Studies in Conversation Analysis* 53–56. Cambridge: Cambridge University Press.

Horváth, Viktória (2004) Megakadásjelenségek a párbeszédekben [Speech disfluencies in dialogues]. In Mária Gósy (ed.) *Beszédkutatás 2004* [Speech Research 2004] 187–199. Budapest: MTA Nyelvtudományi Intézet.

Horváth, Viktória (2007) Vannak-e 'női' és 'férfi' megakadásjelenségek a spontán beszédben? [Are there gender-based differences in disfluency phenomena?] *Magyar Nyelvőr* [Hungarian Purist] 131(3): 315–323.

Huszár, Ágnes (2005) *A gondolattól a szóig: A beszéd folyamata a nyelvbotlások tükrében* [From Thought to Word: The Process of Speech in the Light of the Slips of the Tongue]. Budapest: Tinta Kiadó.

Jasperson, Robert (1998) *Repair after Cut-off.* PhD Dissertation, University of Colorado, Boulder.

Jefferson, Gail (1972) Side sequences. In David Sudnow (ed.) *Studies in Social Interaction* 294–338. New York: Free Press.

Jefferson, Gail (1974) Error correction as an interactional resource. *Language in Society* 3(2): 181–199. https://doi.org/10.1017/S0047404500004334

Jefferson, Gail (1987) On exposed and embedded correction in conversation. In Graham Button and John R. E. Lee (eds.) *Talk and Social Organisation* 86–100. Clevedon, UK: Multilingual Matters.

Jefferson, Gail (2004) Glossary of transcript symbols with an introduction. In Gene H. Lerner (ed.) *Conversation Analysis: Studies from the First Generation* 13–31. Amsterdam: John Benjamins. https://doi.org/10.1075/pbns.125.02jef

Jurafsky, Daniel, Bell, Alan, Fosler-Lussier, Eric, Girand, Cynthia, and Raymond, William (1998) Reduction of English function words in switchboard. In Robert H. Mannell and Jordi Robert-Ribes (eds.) *Proceedings of the International Conference on Spoken Language Processing 7* 3111–3114. Sydney: Australian Speech Science and Technology Association.

Kenesei, István (2000) Szavak, szófajok, toldalékok [Words, word classes, affixes]. In Ferenc Kiefer (ed.) *Strukturális magyar nyelvtan 3* [Structural Hungarian Grammar 3] 75–136. Budapest: Akadémiai Kiadó.

Kertész, András, and Rákosi, Csilla (2012) *Data and Evidence in Linguistics: A Plausible Argumentation Model.* Cambridge: Cambridge University Press. https://doi.org/10. 1017/CBO9780511920752

Kertész, András, and Rákosi, Csilla (2014) *The Evidential Basis of Linguistic Argumentation.* Amsterdam and Philadelphia: John Benjamins Publishing Company. https://doi. org/10.1075/slcs.153

Kiefer, Ferenc (1982) *Az előfeltevések elmélete* [The Theory of Presuppositions]. Budapest: Akadémiai Kiadó.

Kim, Kyu-Hyun (1993) Other-initiated repair sequences in Korean conversation as interactional resources. In Soonja Choi (ed.) *Japanese/Korean Linguistics III* 3–18. Stanford, CA: Center for the Study of Language and Information, Leland Stanford Junior University.

Kim, Kyu-Hyun (2001) Confirming intersubjectivity through retroactive elaboration: Organization of phrasal units in other-initiated repair sequences in Korean conversation. In Margret Selting and Elizabeth Couper-Kuhlen (eds.) *Studies in Interactional Linguistics* 345–372. Amsterdam: John Benjamins. https://doi.org/10.1075/ sidag.10.16kim

Kitzinger, Celia (2013) Repair. In Jack Sidnell and Tanya Stivers (eds.) *The Handbook of Conversation Analysis* 229–256. Oxford: Wiley-Blackwell. https://doi.org/10. 1002/9781118325001.ch12

Kolk, Herman, and Postma, Albert (1997) Stuttering as a covert repair phenomena. In Richard F. Curlee and Gerald M. Siegel (eds.) *Nature and Treatment of Stuttering: New Directions* 182–203. Needham Heights, MA: Allye and Bacon.

Laakso, Minna, and Sorjonen, Marja-Leena (2010) Cut-off or particle: Devices for initiating self-repair in conversation. *Journal of Pragmatics* 42(4): 1151–1172. https:// doi.org/10.1016/j.pragma.2009.09.004

Leech, Geoffrey N. (1983) *Principles of Pragmatics.* London: Longman.

Lehmann, Christian (2004) Data in linguistics. *The Linguistic Review* 21(3–4): 175–210. https://doi.org/10.1515/tlir.2004.21.3-4.175

Lerch, Ágnes (2007) Az ismétlés mint az önjavítás eszköze a magyarban [Repetition as a means of self-repair in Hungarian]. In Tamás Gecső and Csilla Sárdi (eds.) *Nyelvelmélet – nyelvhasználat* [Language Theory and Language Use] 123–130. Budapest: Tinta Könyvkiadó.

Lerner, Gene H. (2013) On the place of hesitating in delicate formulations: A turn-constructional infrastructure for collaborative indiscretion. In Makoto Hayashi, Geoffrey Raymond, and Jack Sidnell (eds.) *Conversational Repair and Human Understanding* 95–134. Cambridge: Cambridge University Press. https://doi.org/10. 1017/CBO9780511757464.004

Levelt, Willem J. M. (1983) Monitoring and self-repair in speech. *Cognition* 14(1): 41–104. https://doi.org/10.1016/0010-0277(83)90026-4

Levelt, Willem J. M. (1989) *Speaking: From Intention to Articulation*. Cambridge, MA: MIT Press.

Levinson, Stephen (2013) Action formation and ascription. In Jack Sidnell and Tanya Stivers (eds.) *The Handbook of Conversation Analysis* 103–130. Oxford: Wiley-Blackwell. https://doi.org/10.1002/9781118325001.ch6

Lipták, Anikó K. (2005) The left periphery of Hungarian exclamatives. In Laura Bruge, Giuliana Giusti, Nicola Munaro, Walter Schweikert, and Giuseppina Turano (eds.) *Contributions to the Thirtieth Incontro di Grammatica Generativa* 161–183. Venice: Cafoscarina.

Luke, Kang-Kwong, and Zhang, Wei (2010) Insertion as a self-repair device and its interactional motivations in Chinese conversation. *Chinese Language and Discourse* 1(2): 153–182. https://doi.org/10.1075/cld.1.2.01luk

Maheux-Pelletier, Genevieve, and Golato, Andrea (2008) Repair in membership categorization in French. *Language in Society* 37(5): 689–712. https://doi.org/10.1017/S0047404508080998

Markó, Alexandra (2004) Megakadások vizsgálata különféle monologikus szövegekben [The examination of speech disfluencies in various monologic texts]. In Mária Gósy (ed.) *Beszédkutatás 2004* [Speech Research 2004] 209–222. Budapest: MTA Nyelvtudományi Intézet.

Markó, Alexandra (2006) A megakadásjelenségek hatása a beszédészlelésre [The effect of disfluency phenomena on speech perception]. *Alkalmazott Nyelvtudomány* [Applied Linguistics] VI/1–2: 103–117.

Moerman, Michael (1977) The preference for self-correction in a Tai conversational corpus. *Language* 53(4): 872–882. https://doi.org/10.2307/412915

Mondada, Lorenza (2013) The conversation analytic approach to data collection. In Jack Sidnell and Tanya Stivers (eds.) *The Handbook of Conversation Analysis* 32–56. Oxford: Wiley-Blackwell. https://doi.org/10.1002/9781118325001.ch3

Moravcsik, Edith A. (1969) *Determination: Working Papers on Language Universals 1*. Stanford University, CA: Committee on Linguistics.

Nagy C., Katalin, Németh T., Enikő, and Németh, Zsuzsanna (2018) Merging various data analysis techniques in pragmatics. *Sprachtheorie und germanistische Linguistik* 28(2): 155–183.

Németh, Zsuzsanna (2007–2008) A forduló (beszédlépés) kiterjesztésének grammatikája a magyarban [The grammatics of turn-expansion in Hungarian]. *Nyelvtudomány III-IV* [Linguistics III-IV]: 149–183.

Németh, Zsuzsanna (2012) Recycling and replacement repairs as self-initiated same-turn self-repair strategies in Hungarian. *Journal of Pragmatics* 44(14): 2022–2034. https://doi.org/10.1016/j.pragma.2012.09.015

Németh, Zsuzsanna (2017) The interactional functions of four repair operations in Hungarian. In Stavros Assimakopoulos (ed.) *Pragmatics at its Interfaces* 279–310. Berlin: Mouton de Gruyter. https://doi.org/10.1515/9781501505089-014

Nooteboom, Sieb G. (1980) Speaking and unspeaking: Detection and correction of phonological and lexical errors in spontaneous speech. In Victoria A. Fromkin (ed.)

Errors in Linguistic Performance: Slips of the Tongue, Ear, Pen, and Hand 87–96. New York: Academic Press.

Nooteboom, Sieb G. (2005) Lexical bias revisited: Detecting, rejecting and repairing speech errors in inner speech. *Speech Communication* 47(1–2): 43–58. https://doi. org/10.1016/j.specom.2005.02.003

O'Neal, George (2015) Segmental repair and interactional intelligibility: The relationship between consonant deletion, consonant insertion, and pronunciation intelligibility in English as a Lingua Franca in Japan. *Journal of Pragmatics* 85(1): 122–134. https://doi. org/10.1016/j.pragma.2015.06.013

Pérez, Elvira, Santiago, Julio, Palma, Alfonso, and O'Seaghdha, Padraig G. (2007) Perceptual bias in speech error data collection: Insights from Spanish speech errors. *Journal of Psycholinguistic Research* 36(3): 207–235. https://doi.org/10.1007/s10936-006-9042-7

Pomerantz, Anita (1978) Compliment responses: Notes on the co-operation of multiple constraints. In Jim Schenkein (ed.) *Studies in the Organization of Conversational Interaction* 79–112. New York: Academic Press. https://doi.org/10.1016/B978-0-12-623550-0.50010-0

Pomerantz, Anita (1986) Extreme case formulations: A way of legitimizing claims. *Human Studies* 9(2–3): 219–229. https://doi.org/10.1007/BF00148128

Pomerantz, Anita, and Heritage, John (2013) Preference. In Jack Sidnell and Tanya Stivers (eds.) *The Handbook of Conversation Analysis* 210–228. Oxford: Wiley-Blackwell. https://doi.org/10.1002/9781118325001.ch11

Postma, Albert (2000) Detection of errors during speech production: A review of speech monitoring models. *Cognition* 77(2): 97–131. https://doi.org/10.1016/S0010-0277(00)00090-1

Postma, Albert, Kolk, Herman H. J., and Povel, Dirk-Jan (1990) On the relation among speech errors, disfluencies, and self-repairs. *Language and Speech* 33(1): 19–29. https:// doi.org/10.1177/002383099003300102

Poulisse, Nanda (1999) *Slips of the Tongue: Speech Errors in First and Second Language Production.* Amsterdam: John Benjamins. https://doi.org/10.1075/sibil.20

Rieger, Caroline L. (2003) Repetitions as self-repair strategies in English and German conversations. *Journal of Pragmatics* 35(1): 47–69. https://doi.org/10.1016/S0378-2166(01)00060-1

Robinson, Jeffrey D. (2006) Managing trouble responsibility and relationships during conversational repair. *Communication Monographs* 73(2): 137–161. https://doi.org/10.1080/03637750600581206

Sacks, Harvey (1987) [1973] On the preferences for agreement and contiguity in sequences in conversation. In Graham Button and John R. E. Lee (eds.) *Talk and Social Organisation* 54–69. Clevedon, UK: Multilingual Matters.

Sacks, Harvey (1995a) [1964–1968] *Lectures on Conversation 1.* Oxford: Blackwell. https:// doi.org/10.1002/9781444328301

Sacks, Harvey (1995b) [1968–1972] *Lectures on Conversation 2.* Oxford: Blackwell.

Sacks, Harvey, Schegloff, Emanuel A., and Jefferson, Gail (1974) A simplest systematics for the organization of turn-taking for conversation. *Language* 50(4): 696–735. https://doi. org/10.1353/lan.1974.0010

Sacks, Harvey, and Schegloff, Emanuel A. (1979) Two preferences in the organization of reference to persons in conversation and their interaction. In George Psathas (ed.) *Everyday Language: Studies in Ethnomethodology* 15–21. New York: Irvington Publishers.

Schegloff, Emanuel A. (1979) The relevance of repair to syntax-for-conversation. In Talmy Givón (ed.) *Syntax and Semantics XII.* 261–286. New York: Academic Press.

Schegloff, Emanuel A. (1987) Recycled turn beginnings, a precise repair mechanism in conversation's turn-taking organization. In Graham Button and John R. E. Lee (eds.) *Talk and Social Organisation* 70–85. Clevedon, UK: Multilingual Matters.

Schegloff, Emanuel A. (1988) On an actual virtual servo-mechanism for guessing bad news: A single case conjecture. *Social Problems* 35(4): 442–457. https://doi.org/10.2307/800596

Schegloff, Emanuel A. (1992) Repair after next turn: The last structurally provided defense of intersubjectivity in conversation. *American Journal of Sociology* 97(5): 1295–1345. https://doi.org/10.1086/229903

Schegloff, Emanuel A. (1993) Reflections on quantification in the study of conversation. *Research on Language and Social Interaction* 26(1): 99–128. https://doi.org/10.1207/s15327973rlsi2601_5

Schegloff, Emanuel A. (1996) Confirming allusions: Toward an empirical account of action. *American Journal of Sociology* 102(1): 161–216. https://doi.org/10.1086/230911

Schegloff, Emanuel A. (1997) Third turn repair. In Gregory R. Guy, Crawford Feagin, Deborah Schiffrin, and John Baugh (eds.) *Towards a Social Science of Language: Papers in Honour of William Labov II* 31–40. Amsterdam: John Benjamins.

Schegloff, Emanuel A. (2000) When 'others' initiate repair. *Applied Linguistics* 21(2): 205–243. https://doi.org/10.1093/applin/21.2.205

Schegloff, Emanuel A. (2007) *Sequence Organization in Interaction: A Primer in Conversation Analysis.* Cambridge: Cambridge University Press. https://doi.org/10.1017/CBO9780511791208

Schegloff, Emanuel A. (2008) *Ten Operations in Self-initiated, Same-Turn Repair.* Paper presented at the conference on repair and intersubjectivity in talk and social interaction, University of Toronto.

Schegloff, Emanuel A. (2009) One perspective on *Conversation Analysis: Comparative Perspectives.* In Jack Sidnell (ed.) *Conversation Analysis: Comparative Perspectives* 357–406. Cambridge: Cambridge University Press. https://doi.org/10.1017/CBO9780511635670.013

Schegloff, Emanuel A. (2013) Ten operations in self-initiated, same-turn repair. In Makoto Hayashi, Geoffrey Raymond, and Jack Sidnell (eds.) *Conversational Repair and Human Understanding* 41–70. Cambridge: Cambridge University Press. https://doi.org/10.1017/CBO9780511757464.002

Schegloff, Emanuel A., Jefferson, Gail, and Sacks, Harvey (1977) The preference for self-correction in the organization of repair in conversation. *Language* 53(2): 361–382. https://doi.org/10.1353/lan.1977.0041

Schenkein, Jim (1978) Sketch of an analytic mentality for the study of conversational interaction. In Jim Schenkein (ed.) *Studies in the Organization of Conversational Interaction* 1–6. New York: Academic Press. https://doi.org/10.1016/B978-0-12-623550-0.50007-0

Schirm, Anita (2011) *A diskurzusjelölők funkciói: A hát, az -e és a vajon elemek története és jelenkori szinkrón státusa alapján* [The functions of discourse markers: on the basis of the history and present status of the elements 'hát', '-e', and 'vajon']. PhD dissertation, University of Szeged. http://doktori.bibl.u-szeged.hu/759/1/schirm_anita_doktori_disszertacio.pdf

Searle, John R. (1969) *Speech Acts.* Cambridge: Cambridge University Press.

Searle, John R. (1975) Indirect speech acts. In Peter Cole and Jerry L. Morgan (eds.) *Syntax and Semantics III* 59–82. New York: Academic Press.

Searle, John R. (1976) A classification of illocutionary acts. *Language in Society* 5(1): 1–24. https://doi.org/10.1017/S0047404500006837

Searle, John R., and Vanderveken, Daniel (1985) *Foundations of Illocutionary Logic.* Cambridge: Cambridge University Press.

Selkirk, Elisabeth (2008) The prosodic structure of function words. In John J. McCarthy (ed.) *Optimality Theory in Phonology: A Reader* 464–482. Oxford: Blackwell. https://doi.org/10.1002/9780470756171.ch25

Shriberg, Elizabeth (2001) To 'errr' is human: Ecology and acoustics of speech disfluencies. *Journal of the International Phonetic Association* 31(1): 153–169. https://doi.org/10.1017/S0025100301001128

Sidnell, Jack (2008) Alternate and complementary perspectives on language and social life: The organization of repair in two Caribbean communities. *Journal of Sociolinguistics* 12(4): 477–503. https://doi.org/10.1111/j.1467-9841.2008.00377.x

Sidnell, Jack (2010) *Conversation Analysis: An Introduction.* Oxford: Wiley-Blackwell. https://doi.org/10.1093/obo/9780199772810-0062

Sidnell, Jack, and Stivers, Tanya (eds.) (2013) *The Handbook of Conversation Analysis.* Oxford: Wiley-Blackwell. https://doi.org/10.1002/9781118325001

Stivers, Tanya (2005) Modified repeats: One method for asserting primary rights from second position. *Research on Language and Social Interaction* 38(2): 131–158. https://doi.org/10.1207/s15327973rlsi3802_1

Stivers, Tanya (2011) Morality and question design: 'Of course' as contesting a presupposition of askability. In Tanya Stivers, Lorenza Mondada, and Jakob Steensig (eds.) *The Morality of Knowledge in Conversation* 82–106. Cambridge: Cambridge University Press. https://doi.org/10.1017/CBO9780511921674.005

Stivers, Tanya (2013) Sequence organization. In Jack Sidnell and Tanya Stivers (eds.) *The Handbook of Conversation Analysis* 191–209. Oxford: Wiley-Blackwell. https://doi.org/10.1002/9781118325001.ch10

Stivers, Tanya, and Robinson, Jeffrey D. (2006) A preference for progressivity in interaction. *Language in Society* 35(3): 367–392. https://doi.org/10.1017/S0047404506060179

Stivers, Tanya, and Sidnell, Jack (2013) Introduction. In Jack Sidnell and Tanya Stivers (eds.) *The Handbook of Conversation Analysis* 1–8. Oxford: Wiley-Blackwell. https://doi.org/10.1002/9781118325001.ch1

Svennevig, Jan (2008) Trying the easiest solution first in other-initiation of repair. *Journal of Pragmatics* 40(2): 333–348. https://doi.org/10.1016/j.pragma.2007.11.007

Szili, Katalin (2000) Az udvariasság elméletéről, megjelenési módjairól a magyar nyelvben [On the theory and appearance of politeness in Hungarian]. *Hungarológia* [Hungarology] 2(1–2): 261–282.

Szili, Katalin (2004) A bókra adott válaszok pragmatikája: Adalékok a szerénység nyelvi megnyilvánulásához a magyar nyelvben [The pragmatics of replies to compliments: Data on the manifestation of the principle of modesty in Hungarian]. *Magyar Nyelvőr* [Hungarian Purist] 128(3): 265–285.

Szili, Katalin (2010) The linguistic forms of modesty in the Hungarian language or the pragmatics of compliment response. In Iwona Witczak-Plisiecka (ed.) *Pragmatic Perspectives on Language and Linguistics* 149–164. Cambridge: Cambridge Scholars Publishing.

Wehmeier, Sally (ed.) (2000) *Oxford Advanced Learner's Dictionary of Current English.* Oxford: Oxford University Press.

Whitehead, Kevin A. (2009) 'Categorizing the categorizer': The management of racial common sense in interaction. *Social Psychology Quarterly* 72(4): 325–342. https://doi.org/10.1177/019027250907200406

Wilkinson, Sue, and Weatherall, Ann (2011) Insertion repair. *Research on Language and Social Interaction* 44(1): 65–91. https://doi.org/10.1080/08351813.2011.544136

Wouk, Fay (2005) The syntax of repair in Indonesian. *Discourse Studies* 7(2): 237–258. https://doi.org/10.1177/1461445605050368

Wu, Ruey-Jiuan Regina (2006) Initiating repair and beyond: The use of two repeat-formatted repair initiations in Mandarin conversation. *Discourse Processes* 41(1): 67–109. https://doi.org/10.1207/s15326950dp4101_5

Index of authors

CPSIA information can be obtained
at www.ICGtesting.com
Printed in the USA
JSHW050434170721
16999JS00004B/13